CONTENTS

CW00976721

Soundings

Frances Angela lives in London. Her poems have been widely published in magazines.

Les Back is Reader in Sociology at Goldsmiths College. His most recent books include *Changing Face of Football: racism, identity and multiculture in the English game* (Berg, 2001) and *Out of Whiteness: color, politics and culture* (University of Chicago, 2002).

Richard Clayton recently left his job at a branding consultancy to become a freelance journalist and critic.

Phil Cohen is Director of the Centre for New Ethnicities Research at the University of East London.

Anne Costello was a member of the London Support Group for the Liverpool Dockers during 1996-97.

Robert Hackett is Co-director of NewsWatch Canada.

Grazyna Kubica works at Jagiellonian University, Krakow and is an Executive Committee Member of the European Association of Social Anthropologists. She co-edited *Malinowski Between Two Worlds* (CUP 1988), and is presently preparing a Polish edition of Malinowski's diaries.

Stuart Hall is a co-editor of *Soundings*.

Les Levidow is Managing Editor of *Science as Culture*. He is co-editor of several books, including *Science, Technology and the Labour Process*; *Anti-Racist Science Teaching*; and *Cyborg Worlds: The Military Information Society* (Free Association Books, 1983, 1987, 1989). He was a member of the London Support Group for the Liverpool Dockers during 1996-97.

Jo Littler is a lecturer in Media and Cultural Studies at Middlesex University.

Linda McDowell teaches human geography at University College, London. She is author of *Gender Identity and Place* (Polity 1999) and is currently writing a book about young men to be called *Redundant Masculinities?*, to be published by Blackwells.

Jonathan Rutherford is a lecturer in Media and Cultural Studies at Middlesex University and author of several books, including *The Art of Life* (2000) and *Young Britain* (1998).

Hisham Matar is a Libyan writer who for the past twenty-one years has been the resident of an elusive and abstract homeland named Exile: at the time of writing, England.

Chantal Mouffe is Research Fellow at the Centre for the Study of Democracy at the University of Westminster. She is the author of several books including *Hegemony and Socialist Strategy: Towards a Radical Democratic Politics*, 1985, revised 2001 (with Ernesto Laclau) and *The Return of the Political*, 1993.

Caroline Price is a violinist and teacher. Her two poetry collections are *Thinking of the Bull Dancers* (Littlewood) and *Pictures Against Skin* (Rockingham Press).

David Slater is Professor of Social and Political Geography at Loughborough University. He is the author of *Territory and State Power in Latin America* (Macmillan 1989) and co-editor of *The American Century* (Blackwell 1999).

Nicholas Waddell recently graduated in history with development studies at the University of Sussex where he was co-ordinator of the Africa Forum - a group for understanding and promoting awareness of issues relevant to contemporary Africa.

Gregory Warren Wilson is a professional violinist. His poetry has won many awards. His latest collection is *Hanging Windchimes in a Vacuum* (1997).

Gary Younge is a journalist with *The Guardian*.

Eli Zaretsky is Professor of History at the New School for Social Research, New York.

Correction:

Matthew Beaumont, a contributor to *Soundings 18*, is an editor of *Historical Materialism*, not *Human Relations*.

Soundings discussions

At the very end of 2001, *Soundings* hosted an evening's discussion on the war in Afghanistan. It was hastily organised in the context of, and in response to, what seemed like a deafening silence over the deeper and more difficult issues raised by the actions of Bush and Blair and the discourses mobilised around them. We had time, also, for only the most minimal of advance advertising. Yet the meeting was packed, and people were having to be turned away from the doors. The debate was complex and thought-provoking, and we are grateful to all those who took part. We open this issue with papers drawn from the opening contributions of that evening: from Stuart Hall, Chantal Mouffe, and Gary Younge.[1] These are followed by further contributions on the crisis from David Slater (another participant in the meeting), Eli Zaretsky and Bob Hackett. Whilst even now the bombing and the 'war against terror' continues and may yet be extended, debate over the some of the bigger issues raised has often been inadequate in the mainstream media, and has sometimes been shied away from altogether.

This was by no means the first time *Soundings* has organised political discussion beyond the pages of the journal itself (for example there have been joint events with *Signs of the Times*, regular Saturday morning seminars, and a series of conferences and meetings on Emotional Labour, following up the theme of Issue Number 11) - and this is activity we want to continue. Events like these help the journal to be more than just a three-times yearly publication, and give stimulus and focus to its thinking. We are now planning a conference on the theme of 'Privatisation and the Public' (temporarily eclipsed by war but never far from everyone's mind). As with suggestions for Themes for future issues, please contact us with suggestions for topics and offers to organise such events.

The rest of this issue continues our established commitment to diversity of topic and style: Jonathan Rutherford contributes a critical essay on the new knowledge economy, and the increasing commodification of intellectual property;

---

1. Thanks to colleagues at *Red Pepper* for providing the tapes of the meeting, and to Sarah Benton for chairing it.

Les Back reflects on some of the miseries still being endured in New Labour Britain; Anne Costello and Les Levidow analyse the neoliberal flexibility agenda, and document some recent struggles against the EU-wide campaign by European business to erode workplace rights in the name of economic competitiveness; Linda McDowell finds that myths about a widespread yob culture serve to conceal some of the very real problems in the complex lives of young working-class men; Grazyna Kubica offers a selection from the diary she kept of her travels in Britain, interspersing them with extracts from the much earlier diaries of Bronislaw Malinowski; and finally there is our usual eclectic selection of poetry and reviews.

The new world disorder

Stuart Hall, Chantal Mouffe and Gary Younge

What follows is a slightly edited transcript of a discussion recently organised by Soundings *to think through some of the issues raised by 11 September.*

Stuart Hall: 'Out of a clear blue sky'

My main purpose is to provoke a discussion rather than to elaborate a fixed position. Therefore I will briefly say something under a number of headings which seem to me to be critical for a rounded approach. I do this by putting questions to myself.

The first one is: is 11 September and the succeeding events an absolutely new phenomenon? Was it something staggeringly novel? Does it change everything?

My answer is that there are certain very important new elements but it is not an absolutely new phenomenon. Dramatic events do make it seem as if nothing will ever be the same again, but when you stand back from them you see that the elements that are now in play - although not appearing in exactly the form that one has seen before - are not unfamiliar. They relate to things we have been worrying about and thinking about for a very long period of time. So there is this curious effect of something which is both familiar and strange, both an event - a rupture - and a kind of unveiling of some of the huge consequences of long-running processes that were always-already in place

The next question is: is terrorism a viable political strategy? Perhaps 'viability' is not the issue. It probably is viable, and it's certainly effective - but is it a political strategy which can deliver profound social change? My answer to that is probably not. Besides, I am opposed on moral grounds to terrorism of the kind that is at issue here - that is to say, violence which is completely unfocused, directed against civilian populations, and with the express purpose of stimulating terror, fear and anxiety in the population.

But I am perfectly well aware - and this is not a quibble - that to discuss the precise limit between terrorism, on the one hand, and legitimate forms of violent resistance to oppression, on the other, is a perfectly appropriate - indeed necessary - debate to have. Unless one is a philosophical pacifist - and I am not - it is necessary to specify what the difference is between the terrorism we saw on 11 September and all sorts of other forms of resistance which have been - and remain - on the political agenda. That is an area which urgently needs discussing.

I am opposed to the definition of terrorism which sweeps up everything together, because once that happens we are facing not a legal or political argument, but an ideological campaign to damn, to demonise, whatever is the political response we don't approve. I remind you of the ANC and armed struggle, and of the even more difficult case of Hisbullah, which is not the same as some of the other so-called terrorist movements, like Hamas, in Palestine: Hisbullah is located in the Lebanon and it is a genuine resistance to Israeli colonisation in that area. It's not a quibble to ask exactly what you mean when you speak of terrorism.

The response which suggests that all terrorism is irrational does not seem to me to be at all helpful. In the context of the massive concentration of the means of violence and other forms of power, terrorism is one of the weapons of the weak, one of the ways in which weak powers can strike back, at the interstices of a system which they define as oppressive. That is not to legitimate it but to try to understand what it is about. The question then cannot be exclusively about terrorism. We must also ask 'was it a legitimate response to real oppression?'

There is much to be said for Edward Said's position, which is that it is time for secular people on the left to say that there is something particularly dangerous about the combination of technology and fundamentalism. That is to say, the means of the delivery of violence without cost, combined with the messianic capacity to mobilise around a kind of absolute, is a very dangerous combination. That is not to say that there is only one kind of fundamentalism in operation.

Finally, if you ask me what ought to have happened after 11 September: I am opposed to what has happened, in particular the indiscriminate bombing of the population of Afghanistan and the rush to unsanctioned violence. I would say it would have been important to define the terrorism of that moment as a crime against humanity - that is to say, to attempt to pursue it and its perpetrators with a genuine form of justice. That would have required some form of international justice by which it could be judged, and some process which could have suspended the definition of who was responsible until proper evidence had been gathered. I am not suggesting this would have been easy - it was inevitable that the Americans would want to see some sort of immediate response. But the dangerous point which we have arrived at now is that, whenever difficult situations like this arise, the fragile means by which some international order could be put together of a more democratic type - that is to say, recourse to the United Nations, the International Court of Human Rights, or the International Court of Justice, citing arguments against violence against the person, etc - are quickly circumvented, left behind, bypassed. What we have instead are responses which take the form of temporary, ad-hoc coalitions of the powerful - like the coalition that fought the Gulf War. They provide convenient cover or legitimation for the rule of law to be sidelined. This is fully in keeping with current American policy, which has deliberately weakened the UN and steadfastly refused to join the project to construct an international court of justice.

The next set of questions I want to ask is: is it the West against Islam? To this I want to say only two things.

The first is that it isn't yet, but it is rapidly becoming that. It is a self-fulfilling prophecy; calculated to produce exactly the result that it claims to be trying to avoid.

The second thing is that it is not a war against Islam: but that doesn't require us to say that every way in which Muslim people respond to the crisis is by definition always okay. I want to identify three aspects - and I say this in friendship to my Muslim friends - in which I find that response inadequate. It is inadequate to quote the Qur'an. All the world religions say we ought to get on with our neighbours. It is a predominant theme in the Bible. But this has never prevented one set of Christians from hacking other Christians and other peoples to death, while quoting the Bible. The whole point about fundamentalism is that you can always find something in the Bible to quote as you destroy your enemy. So it doesn't help to tell me that the Qur'an, like the Bible, says don't hit them.

Secondly, it is not enough to say that all Muslims are brothers. The Muslim world, like every other, is deeply divided by oppositions, between secular versus religious trends, between different interpretations of the holy word. Muslims have themselves to face the fact that the appeal across the board to a universal umma does not correspond to the real world. It is a kind of evasion of the real world. This is not a legitimation of the attacks against Afghanistan. It's simply to say that Muslims who take the position I take - namely, that I'm opposed to the Taliban *and* to the attacks launched by al Qaida, and I don't think Afghanistan should be bombed to smithereens - would be strengthened in their case if they explicitly recognised internal conflicts within Islam itself. Without that, it seems to me, we can't strike effective alliances with them.

L et me ask one more, very broad question, and deal with three or four aspects of it very quickly. I want to look at the notion, which is very widespread in the US and quite widespread in Britain, that to ask the question 'can we understand what is going on' is by definition to defend it. I reject this notion completely. On a recent edition of the news programme *Newsnight*, I heard the proposition advanced that, because the hijackers were middle-class and Osama bin Laden is rich, poverty and terrorism had nothing whatever to do with one another. But not even the Prime Minister thinks that. Instead, he holds to an almost equally empty proposition, that Britain can make globalisation into a 'force for good' around the world. This is an absurd, owlish, position.

I want to argue that there are multiple connections between questions of world poverty and the question of terrorism. And it behoves us at this moment to try to understand why people feel as they do - why people in the Muslim world feel driven to take the kinds of actions they have taken - and not to dismiss their acts as forms of irrationalism.

So what are the constituent elements of such an understanding?

The first point I'd make under that heading is that this seems to me to be the first crisis of the new world disorder - that is to say, of the world of the single superpower which emerged after the cold war. It has many connections with the forms which global conflict assumed during the cold war, but it is radically different, in the sense that in those days, local and smaller scale conflicts were subsumed into the rivalry between the two camps, and this polarisation set some limits on how far local conflicts were allowed to escalate towards their nuclear resolution. The moment of the 'new world order' is the moment of one superpower, the moment of US hegemony. It's the moment of the inauguration of neoliberal forms of globalisation which underpin that hegemony - not just as an economic system but as a political and cultural system. So let's talk about the sources of conflict generated by the new world order of US-dominated neoliberal globalisation.

In this period, the power of the transnational corporations has combined with the power of the United States and other western forces to constitute new international forms of sovereignty for the stabilisation of global power - through organisations like the IMF and the WTO. This *is* a new form of global power. The argument in Negri and Hardt's new book *Empire* is that this is a form of power which has no centre - it's simply a dispersed form because the rule of capital is everywhere and nowadays nothing is outside it. I don't believe this is an accurate picture. I think it does effectively grasp the global interdependence of the nature of power and the nature of the new forms of sovereignty which are arising with neoliberal globalisation, but it doesn't sufficiently recognise the degree to which this global system does still depend on the capacity for forceful intervention by certain dominant nation states like the United States, and - less significantly - the EU or Western Europe. It's a combination of regional power, based on the so-called declining nation states, which have been able to generalise their power effectively through such institutions as the WTO and the IMF, into a kind of unequal global regime.

The distortions of wealth, opportunity, goods, symbolic power, culture, between the South and the North, the gap between the possibilities of life in the North, broadly speaking, and the depth of abandonment in many sections in the South, have been growing steadily over this whole period. The gap has been deepening with globalisation itself, and this has in effect created on the one hand that sense which we found in the United States that somehow its 'homeland' was invulnerable to any fallout from the whole of the rest of the world, and on the other hand that deepening sense of desperation and exclusion in a large part of the rest of the world.

There are two faces of this American power - the haven of hedonism at home, and the intervention overseas, in one sphere after another: its dominance of the organisations that govern economic life, its generation of a globally circulating culture which undermines and unpacks the traditional defences of older societies, without putting anything effective in its place. This is a system of penetrative power, the reverse side of which is the feeling of rage at the multiple ways in which power is exercised against people, and a feeling of profound impotence. We cannot understand the response of the Muslim world to the spectacle of the most powerful nation in the world bombing to smithereens this country which has already been decimated by three previous wars, unless we understand why the spectacle of wealth on the one hand and destitution on the other drives people crazy. It drives them to do things which don't keep to the rules, which are outside the slow processes of reform and moderation which are the forms of political change which we are accustomed to in the West - these processes don't touch them. The weight of debt in Pakistan is not touched by the internal gerry-manderings of power inside the western states. This is the new reality of the world as a whole.

A n event of this kind convenes all those effects in one place. It strips the world of the facades and the boundaries, the invisible walls we put up, between us and knowing what is going on on the other side. We take part in movements against the debt - but we don't really understand what it is like to live with debt. We don't understand what it is like to have the United States, a tremendously productive power, simply dump on us - undercutting local prices - the products of its agri-business, as it does throughout the world. Take the case of Jamaica. Jamaica had a small indigenous dairy industry. But now nobody out there who is poor any longer drinks fresh milk. They drink American powdered milk. The dairy industry has been destroyed because it was worth it for the United States to dump powdered milk into this market simply in order to change habits. There's no distinction here between the culture of the people on the ground, the rules of the IMF and the interests of American global corporations.

To take another example - last year there were blackouts in several third-world cities - Johannesburg, Jaipur, Kingston, Salvador in Brazil. Why? Because over the last year there has been systematic pressure from international forces to put up the public utilities for competition, privatise them and sell them off to private utility corporations in the US, who then drive up the unit costs of electricity and deregulate supply. Do you have any idea of the number of rice farmers in the world who shortly will not be able to plant a fertile seed of rice for next year's crop? It's simply been colonised by the new GM merchants. Now you can go on with a system like this for some time - until at some point something gives. The WTO is currently meeting for a third round of negotiations. But do you think they are going to open the trade barriers to the rest of the world? - 'please compete with us, please make cheap drugs for Aids in South Africa if you're suffering from Aids'. Do you think the pharmaceutical companies have gone to Qatar to offer Aids victims in South Africa generic anti-Aids drugs? High on the agenda (subsequently postponed but not abandoned) are the new competition rules which, with the proposed General Agreement on Services, are designed to oblige all public services - health, education, water, power, transport - to be put up for private sector tender. Tony Blair keeps saying that globalisation can be a force for good, but meanwhile Britain plays an active part in this continued exploitation of the rest of the world.

The Middle East is one of the areas that has been subjected in this period to what Michael Mann recently called exclusionary or 'ostracising' imperialism. And one aspect of the process of destruction has been the maintenance in power of some of the most corrupt and dictatorial political regimes ever seen: our friends - a succession of military regimes in Pakistan; our friends - the Saudi Arabian royal family; our former mate Saddam Hussein; the friend of our friends the Pakistan security forces - Osama bin Laden … This is the way in which this structure has protected itself through its regular and systematic interventions in the world.

And suddenly, out of this seething cauldron, two planes fly into what is the most obvious symbol that any Hollywood producer could ever have selected to symbolise global capitalism at work and play - the twin towers of the World Trade Centre. And we say, hands on our hearts, 'we don't know where they came from. They seemed to come out of a clear blue sky …'

Chantal Mouffe: The disappearance of politics

I agree with Stuart that what we are witnessing is the first example of a crisis of the new world disorder. I am going to centre my intervention around a different aspect, but I would like to indicate at the outset that I am not against the war for pacifist reasons. I am not a pacifist and I believe that in certain circumstances it is necessary to go to war. The problem with this so-called 'war on terrorism' is that it is likely to achieve exactly the contrary of what is intended. It will increase anti-americanism and it will lead to more terrorist acts.

What is particularly worrying is the total refusal by the United States to try to understand why this attack happened. They do not even allow this question to be posed because they consider that trying to understand is automatically to justify. This is has precluded all possibility of debate. As Susan Sontag has said, debate is automatically seen as dissent and dissent as treason. This has created a very perverse dynamics.

The only thing which is allowed is moral condemnation of terrorism in all its forms (except of course for the state terrorism of the Israeli government!). Even on the left many people have limited themselves to a denunciation of terrorism without trying to tackle its causes. It's as if the whole of American society has suddenly become incapable of critical reflection. Bush has become a hero and people are ready to accept the curtailment of their more basic liberties in order to defend the 'American way of life'.

The big originary mistake was probably, as Sir Michael Howard has argued, to have defined the situation as one of war and not as a police operation against criminals. Once it was defined as war, a certain type of rhetoric was automatically mobilised and the possibility of a serious discussion was foreclosed. So we have been presented with a 'crusade of good against evil', a struggle of civilisation against its enemies, and told that 'those who are not with us are against us', by Bush and his deputy Tony Blair.

What I would like to stress is that this moralistic discourse, far from being completely new, is in fact the culmination of a general trend that we have been witnessing for some time in contemporary politics. It is another example of the incapacity in which we find ourselves today of thinking in political terms. This was already true before this crisis and the crisis has simply exacerbated the situation.

This incapacity of envisaging the problems facing contemporary societies through political categories is not limited to the West. It is found worldwide, albeit in different forms. The growth of Islamic fundamentalism is of course one of its better known manifestations, but Islam is certainly not the only religion which is used as a substitute for political discourse and we find similar cases in other religions. The demise of secular ideologies like nationalism and communism has left a void which is increasingly occupied by politicised religious discourses. Of course, as many commentators have pointed out, in many countries this has been promoted by the very elites in power who saw this as a way to weaken the democratic forces and to provide an outlet for the discontent of the masses.

In western countries this disappearance of a properly political discourse has generally taken a different form. Here discourses like the 'Third Way' and the 'Neue Mitte' have evacuated politics of its adversarial component, as choices about alternative ways of organising social relations have been declared outdated. The delegitimation of the conflict between left and right, which is often hailed as a great advance for democracy, has eliminated the very possibility of a democratic challenge to the hegemony of neo-liberalism. Neo-liberal globalisation is perceived as a fate to which we all have to submit, and every attempt to challenge this model is presented as a rejection of 'civilisation'.

We need to understand that when politics ceases to be the place where conflict can be expressed in a society, and when opposition to the existing structure of power cannot find political channels, then this opposition will tend to take other forms. Some of them will be violent; others, while not violent, might nevertheless jeopardise democratic institutions. This is, for instance, the case with the growth of right-wing populist movements. I have for some time been trying to grasp the reasons for their increasing success in Western Europe and I have come to the conclusion that it is linked to the lack of real alternatives to the present order. Indeed in many countries the 'consensus at the centre' has led to a lack of an effective opposition within the spectrum of traditional democratic parties. The only way to express opposition to the dominant order is through right-wing populist movements, which have skilfully managed to articulate resentment towards the political elites by mobilising the theme of popular sovereignty.

The reaction to the rise of right-wing populism has overwhelmingly been a moralistic one. The answer of the traditional parties, of the 'good democrats', has been one of moral condemnation. They have not attempted to understand why those movements have developed, what responsibility they themselves have had for their emergence, or what changes need to be made in order to fight them. In other words, instead of a political response, the kind of discourse that we hear is the following: we are the good democrats and we will establish a cordon sanitaire against the extreme right; we have nothing with which to reproach ourselves, they are the bad ones which need to be destroyed; we should never talk to them, in order not to be contaminated; it is a sort of moral plague that simply needs to be eradicated without any need to critically examine its causes.

I was really struck to find exactly the same kind of discourse in reaction to 11 September. Instead of apprehending the situation in political terms we had again this moralistic scenario of a fight of 'good Americans' against evil 'terrorists', in this case elevating the struggle to a defence of 'civilisation', which is of course identified with the American way of life. We are so good, says Bush, how could people want to harm us! They must be thoroughly evil to be against us. And so of course must be - according to this view - all those who dare to suggest that there might be some other kind of explanation, thereby blaming the victims for this tragedy.

I find the current incapacity to think in political terms extremely dangerous. It renders us unable to grasp the different challenges we are facing and impedes envisaging effective ways of dealing with the numerous crises arising from the new

Soundings

world disorder described by Stuart. As long as the 'no alternative' dogma is not
shattered, the hegemony of neo-liberalism will go on imposing its model of
globalisation as the only legitimate order, describing its opponents as the enemies
of progress and of civilisation. Without any legitimate alternative political discourse,
it is very likely that all the resentment linked to the growing polarisation in the
world will be increasingly channelled through movements which will exacerbate
antagonisms and resort to violent means.

L et me end by saying something about what we could do, even if it is at a
very modest level, to contribute to a revival of political discourse. In the
last years we have witnessed the emergence of a movement, sometimes called
the anti-globalisation movement, but more adequately referred to as the anti-corporate
movement. On the whole its aims have so far been mainly defensive, centring on
protests against the policies of transnational institutions like the World Trade
Organisation (WTO) and the World Bank. But since Porto Alegre in January 2001,
it has begun to tackle the question of what could be an alternative form of
globalisation, and this is a very promising move. I think that the current crisis
represents a defining moment for this movement. On one side there is the danger
that its opponents will manage to create a backlash against it by presenting it as an
objective ally of the terrorists. This strategy is already well under way and it could be
fatal for the movement. If this type of articulation between anti-corporate struggle
and terrorism succeeds in imposing itself, it will be the end not only of the movement
but also of any attempt to envisage how to fight the conditions which are creating a
favourable terrain for terrorism. On the other hand, there is also the possibility for
this movement to articulate its struggle in such a way that its objectives would be
recognised as providing an important dimension in the fight against terrorism. In
that case it could increase its audience and gain a real legitimacy. So I think that it is
very important to emphasise this aspect of the anti-corporate struggle and to stress
how it could contribute to create the conditions which will make it more difficult for
terrorism to flourish. This is a truly decisive moment for this movement because the
articulation could go either way. And we intellectuals and political activists may play
our part in determining the outcome of this hegemonic struggle.

Gary Younge: A world full of gangsters
I'm going to start with 10 September rather than 11 September, and two of the
news stories of 10 September. One can become quite cynical about news, but both

of these stories hit me in a way in which the news normally doesn't - even before 11 September.

The first was - if we can call our minds back to then - a boatload of Afghan refugees floating off Australia. It is interesting now that they should have been Afghans, given that Australia is very involved in the coalition now, and thinks there is nothing better than a liberated Afghanistan and is prepared to send its bombs to liberate Afghanistan. But when people actually came to Australia from Afghanistan, after a treacherous journey, and having almost died, Australia said that they wouldn't let them in. Interesting also that we now have a Foreign Secretary who compares Afghanistan to the Nazis, but who, when he was Home Secretary and a group of Afghans landed at Stanstead, said that there was no fear of persecution there and sent them back.

What we had there was a country which was bound by international law to take those people but who decided that it just didn't want to. Ninety per cent of Australians said 'we don't want 'em', so the Australians felt very gung-ho about not taking the refugees. I remember hearing Mary Robinson on the radio, being asked what could be done, given that they were breaking international law, and she said - well nothing really, all we can do is put moral pressure on them. And the interviewer pointed out that 90 per cent of Australians supported the decision and she said 'That is a problem'. And so, right enough, those refugees were forced to bob around in the most degrading circumstances until they were parked on a desert island.

Around the same time there was also the United Nations conference on racism, and during that time there, once again, there was a most disgraceful display by America and Britain, and much of the rest of the west, in just refusing to acknowledge the legacy of slavery and colonialism. I think it was someone in the Belgian delegation who said, 'Of course we understand that slavery is wrong now, but that doesn't mean that it has always been wrong'.

Interesting really - because what it illustrated is how far the international situation had degraded on 10 September. Before that day I had been in Zimbabwe, where the land occupations were going on and the world was coming down in a big way on Zimbabwe. But the world was not coming down in a big way on the land grabs taking place around the West Bank and Gaza Strip. And there was no attempt even to square these circles. There was a sense among the Western powers that they didn't have to explain themselves actually - because it was not in their interests to explain themselves.

The world on 10 September was a lawless place - it was full of gangsters - and if international law was inconvenient for you then you simply bypassed it and said 'well, we're doing the right thing anyway'. And time and time again we kept seeing this. A vivid example is the massive battle that South African activists - I think it was activists rather than the Government - had to wage to remove the patents on those Aids drugs, and the obstruction of the British and American governments. Compare that to the American government's insistence, as soon as their country was going to be hit with Anthrax, that the patents for the drugs to treat it were removed - and the force with which they could do that.

So what we had on 10 September was a world in which everyone understood - the poor countries understood it and the wealthy countries understood it - that might was right, that wealth and power determined not just economics but morality, politics, and every other thing that could possibly be negotiated in the international arena.

And that brings us on to 11 September and that bewilderment that some Americans - and some other people - have: why us? And one starts from the understanding, where else would they go? They want to fly these planes into a big building, a massive act of situationism, where are they going to go - Stockholm? Somewhere in Canada? At the end of the day there are really only two places if that's what you're looking for. They are going to go either to America or Britain, almost certainly.

And the real issue about 11 September - and this is something I am still computing, this is work in progress - the real issue is scale. Nobody suggested after the bombings of the embassies in 1998 that we were moving into a new world order, that the world would never be the same again, and that's partly because it was mostly Africans who were killed and it was abroad, but it's also because of the scale of the event.

And then one looks at what you mean by scale - and scale is vital to this debate because it informs what you mean by a proportionate response - proportionate to what? Now the only two things I can limit this down to are, first numbers, and then time frame.

The numbers game is an interesting game. It's a filthy game because once one starts dealing with numbers - that, well, only such and such a number of people died so therefore it's all right - that is a completely bankrupt place to be. But nonetheless if we are talking about scale and proportionate response, then numbers have got to be looked at. The numbers killed on 11 September in New York are now - people quoted 6000 at first - estimated at about 2800 as far as I am aware. And in Britain - I know because I wrote the story - they were saying that about 450 Britons were killed when I first went to America, about four days afterwards - the mid 400s - and that's now down to about 80. As these numbers fall we hear less and less of them, but that's about the numbers we are talking about. And then we have to think about countries like Rwanda, like Congo, like Angola - it was more than a million in Congo and Rwanda. So clearly it's not numbers that are the issue, because the world didn't change when all those people in Rwanda were killed.

So then one must ask what is left then, and the only other thing I could think of is time - they all died at the same time. So then you ask yourself in what kind of time frame would it be reasonable for 2000 people to die, for there not to be a change in the world order. And you see that also when you talk about time and scale it's nonsense. So what we're left with when we talk about scale are two things really. First of all it was on television, it all happened live, it was a global event. It was a horrible horrible nasty vicious event but it was also a show and people watched that show again and again and again. And a lot of the world has television, and anyone who has access to a television saw that time and time again. So its scale was in terms of the numbers of people that that reached. The scale was also the fact that it happened in New York, in the heart of a media saturated society, and a society whose media dominates world communications. But even after conceding this, it is hard to avoid the conclusion that the impact of the events was something to do with their happening to Americans.

I want to also make a brief comment on the issue of how the crisis is impacting on racial debate here: it's really knocked us back in many ways - it's knocked the discourse back to about 1985-6. There's a new Tebbit test now - but it's not with cricket but with war, and Muslims are the focus of it. Here's Hugo Young, from my own great organ: 'Do all citizens of migrant stock, particularly Muslims, actually want to be a full member of the society in which they live?', he asks. And then there is Melanie Phillips in the *Sunday Times* asking more or less the same question but admitting that, 'Of course Muslims are as entitled to question or criticise the bombing campaign as are the Labour MPs ... [that's very nice of her] ... but their opinions call into question their very identification as British citizens'. So what you have there - and it goes all the way round the block, there's a piece in the *Telegraph* saying a very similar thing - is a perceived mismatch - an idea which I thought had gone - a dissonance between race and place. And now we have a dissonance between face and place, where you can't be an honest true Muslim and be a British citizen, it would seem.

So in many ways - talking about 'host communities' and how Muslims get on with 'host communities' - there's been a real knockback there. And in particular, many Muslims feel that it is very difficult to protect themselves, and in this atmosphere - I've been calling around quite a lot of people in the last few days for a story I'm doing and they are telling me this - quite a lot of people just aren't going out of the house. I think that's quite a common thing - or they're wearing different clothes so as not to be recognised as Muslims.

Finally, on the question which people ask about what our solution is, where are the ideas coming from to challenge this new disorder. I think one must first of all recognise that the coalition haven't got a clue about what they are doing. To a certain extent - but only to an extent - I think it's okay to simply say, it's not what they are doing now. Even by their own criteria, it's not working, so we've got to think of something else. But on the question of intervention I would like to say, 'if only you didn't intervene ever'. If the Americans hadn't intervened in the Middle East, Israel would not have the military capacity that it has. In Rwanda, Hutus and Tutsis were western constructs. So in answer to the question 'Do you want the west to go in or not?' I would say we want the West to clear up the mess they have made and then we would like them to get out. And in general, as a rule of thumb - though not in every single circumstance - I would say that if only you hadn't intervened, the world would be a safer place. If the west, and the Russians, hadn't intervened in Afghanistan in the way they did from the 1970s, maybe things would be different. This is not to say that the west is responsible for all the ills in the world, but it does mean that they have contributed to a lot of them - because they can. And that is why the west is the west, and why it is wealthy and the South is not.

Perry Anderson, the United States, and the present world conjuncture

Eli Zaretsky

Eli Zaretsky argues that a better understanding of the nature of history and politics in the United States would be useful in the current crisis.

The destruction of the World Trade Centre and the attack on the US Pentagon have underscored the depth of the antagonism felt toward the United States, at least in some parts of the world. At the same time, the attacks have brought to light the international character of the US's support, and the pride, admiration, and, in some cases, love, it inspires, even among its critics. Understanding this duality would take us a long way toward understanding the world in which we live. Such an understanding would focus on an interconnected set of problems that the left has avoided since its nineteenth century birth: understanding the United States as a unique society in its own right, as an engine of international capitalism, and as an horizon on the global imaginary.

Given the importance of such an understanding to the analysis of global politics, one can only welcome Anderson's recent *New Left Review* editorials, especially

'Testing Formula Two' (*NLR* 8, Mar/Apr 2001), which centres on the impeachment of Clinton and the United States 2000 election, and 'Scurrying Toward Bethlehem' (*NLR* 10, Jul/Aug 2001), which, though primarily about Israel, also elaborates Anderson's views concerning US foreign policy. Written with the author's characteristic brilliance, verve, and lucidity, these editorials have the merit of situating the United States in the context of global capitalism as a whole, especially in the context of the decomposition of Keynesianism that began in the 1970s. Nonetheless, they are based on fundamental misunderstandings concerning American society, politics and history; such misunderstandings prevent any adequate comprehension of the present global conjuncture, and thus a critical response to them is required. This article, originally a response to Perry Anderson's recent writing on the US, is a contribution to the debate about the nature of the US role in the world that is currently needed.

Anderson's guiding theme is the struggle for hegemony in the Western political world since the 1970s. In his view, there have been two phases to this struggle. The first, that of the 1980s, witnessed 'pioneering' neo-liberal forces, led by Thatcher and Reagan, which 'chang[ed] the relation of forces between capital and labour' and 'crush[ed] resistance to a new order'. The second, that of Clinton and Blair in the 1990s, Anderson terms 'regimes of consolidation'. They accepted and extended the legacy of the pioneers, but did not substantially modify it. In both phases, however, the neo-liberal focus on the market was too 'abstract and arid' for mass politics; hence hegemony required an 'ideological supplement'. In the case of Reagan, this supplement was fundamentalist religion; in the case of Thatcher, national chauvinism. In both cases, the supplement led to trouble. Thus, the Clinton and Blair regimes sought to avoid 'any sharp ideological edges', nursing their supporters with the 'soothing emulsion' of 'the third way'.

In 'Testing Formula Two', the thrust of this schema is to minimise the significance of the Clinton Presidency and to narrow the differences between Gore and Bush. Accordingly, Anderson argues against the US left's interpretation of the 2000 election. In particular, he argues against the following widespread views: that the 2000 election was 'stolen' by the Republicans; that Gore's failure to win decisively lay in his personality and in his refusal to identify himself with Clinton's achievements; and that the election of Bush represented a real danger to democratic forces, both in the US and in the world at large. In their place, Anderson argues that the Democrats would have behaved exactly as the Republicans did, given

Bush's initial 323 vote lead; that Gore rightly followed polls in distancing himself from Clinton; and that the Bush Presidency was 'unlikely to alter the status quo at home very much', and was preferable to Gore in regard to foreign policy, since it was likely to follow a non-interventionist role, for example in the Balkans and in Israel. The key mistake of the American left, according to Anderson, lay in its failure to support the impeachment of Clinton. For him, impeachment was clearly warranted and would have led directly to the election of Gore.

Needless to say, Anderson's reliability as a prognosticator lies shattered by events. In its first few short months - until the events of 11 September - the Bush Presidency wreaked substantial havoc both on the American economy and on international stability, however stability is understood. Only those who would follow the old Communist idea (which is not Anderson's) that the worse things get, the better for the left, could welcome the extraordinary problems that began to show themselves before 11 September. Domestically, these included the long-term paralysis of the US government's ability to influence the economy as a result of the Bush tax-cut, an opening attempt to isolate labour, and the beginnings of an attack on the right to abortion. Internationally, Bush stood for unilateralism, not non-interventionism: withdrawal from the Kyoto treaty, as well as numerous other international agreements (including one regulating biological weapons); the destruction of the movement toward normalisation in Korea; the weakening of US relations with China and, at first, Russia; the insistence on the missile defence; in short, a wholesale attack on the internationalist tradition in American foreign policy. Nonetheless, prognostication is no test of analytic value, at least in the world of human affairs, and faulty predictions are not the main problem with Anderson's account.

Anderson's arguments also sometimes reflect a relative unfamiliarity with US history. For example, the US Constitution reserves impeachment for 'high crimes and misdemeanours'. Anderson concludes that this standard justifies Clinton's impeachment, based on Clinton's 'sexual molestation' and the possibility that he perjured himself. (And it is only a possibility, as such a case would have to be established legally, something that would be difficult considering the triviality of his offence and the fact of entrapment, both relevant to a conviction for perjury.) But 'misdemeanour' meant a serious issue of state in the eighteenth century, whereas today it covers even traffic infractions. Similarly, Anderson pooh-poohs the danger of Bush's judicial appointments and calls the Republican right a 'paper tiger', suggesting that the abortion issue is a settled matter in

American politics; but this suggestion is belied by Bush's stem-cell manoeuvring and attack on funding for international institutions that pay for abortions. Nonetheless, like mistaken predictions, errors of fact are inevitable. Again, the problems with Anderson's analysis run deeper.

There are two basic problems with Anderson's account. The first lies in his conception of hegemony as a struggle over marketisation. While basically correct, his approach is unmediated. For both the proponents of neo-liberalism and its critics, matters of race, culture, religion and the meaning of modernity are central; they are not 'ideological supplements'. In the case of the United States, I will argue that many of the debates on these issues centred on a difference over the nature of the Presidency (not merely which party filled the office). Furthermore, globalisation and foreign policy are issues of domestic politics in which culture and economics are inevitably entwined.

Anderson's second problem lies in his one-sided opposition to America's global role. As I will also show, he wants a world in which America's global influence is as limited as possible. But this is neither possible nor desirable. In general, universal ideals such as, in our time, individual freedom, women's emancipation, or respect for cultural differences, do not propagate themselves in ether. Rather, religions, empires, and cultural explosions carry them, albeit in partial, compromised, but concrete forms. Rome, China, Islam, and Britain in the nineteenth century, all offer examples. The United States in our time is simply too big, and in many ways too positive a force, to be contained within Anderson's narrow compass. Anderson's failure to understand this vitiates his account of the global conjuncture.

Both of Anderson's difficulties can be seen in his analysis of the American Presidency. According to Anderson the reason the US left supported Clinton against his impeachers was that it succumbed to a 'cult of the Presidency', a cult that has turned the US left into an appendage of the Democratic Party, and has justified interventions, for example in Kosovo and the Middle East, that Anderson opposes. According to him, the US left should return to the 'founding fathers'' 'Enlightenment-inspired' conception of a 'modest' Presidency. The conviction of Clinton would have signalled such a return, and would have also justified retroactively the calls for impeachment in the Watergate and Iran-Contra affairs. The 'cult of the presidency', according to Anderson, is a cold war relic, a swaggering imperial president who stands astride the globe. The US left should abandon this cult.

Anderson fundamentally misconstrues the nature of the Presidency. *Pace* Anderson, the writers of the Constitution did not envision a 'modest' Presidency; rather, they put the President in place of the King. Indeed, whereas in parliamentary systems, such as in the United Kingdom, the monarch or President divides authority with a Prime Minister, in the United States, the President is simultaneously chief executive officer and symbol of national unity. However, the original purpose of the President's enormous authority was not justice but order. Indeed, as William Lloyd Garrison argued in the nineteenth century, and as David Brion Davis has recently reiterated, slavery, and everything slavery required in terms of authority, hierarchy and order, was at the heart of the original Constitution.

It is true that the US left's support for Clinton in the impeachment struggle rested on its perception of the importance of a powerful Presidency. This, however, was not because it was spellbound by a 'cult', but rather because the impeachment awoke it to the fact that in the course of American history, the office had been transformed to become the chief focus of democratic aspirations. In what could be called its second birth, the Presidency was supposed to be guided by considerations of justice, even when, as in the case of the Civil War, the sit-down strikes, or the Civil Rights movement, justice conflicted with order. This second Presidency was especially important to outsiders and subordinate groups: immigrants, African-Americans, and in our day, women and homosexuals. It was precisely because these groups perceived Clinton as their champion that they supported him, and understood that the Republican attempt to impeach him had nothing to do with 'misdemeanours'.

Anderson ignores the significance of African-American support for Clinton and Gore. The true foundational moment of what I have called the second Presidency was the Civil War. In the presidential campaign of 1860, Abraham Lincoln argued, against Stephen Douglas, that the nation had to take a stand on a fundamental moral issue, namely slavery. Douglas, reflecting the standpoint of the framers of the Constitution, and anticipating today's Republicans, argued that different states could take different positions. Douglas lost the debate, and the Confederates lost the Civil War. It is true that it was not until the 1890s that presidential powers began to expand, but the link between the national government and justice was forged during the struggle over slavery. Bush's repeated insistence that his goal was the restoration of order ('the *tone* in Washington'), and not to use the Presidency to advance the cause of justice, was a direct attack on this legacy.

Anderson minimises the differences between the Democratic and Republican parties. In doing so, he fails to appreciate the importance that the Confederacy plays in American history. Even though it lost the battles, the Confederacy won a spectacular ideological victory after the Civil War in denying the role of slavery. The Republicans are the heirs to that victory. While the Party began as an anti-slavery party, its hegemony after 1877 rested on its acceptance of racial subordination. During the 1930s it became the party of opposition to the Presidency and to the federal government, the only force that could (and did) counter racial oppression. The party's true, modern birth lies in the desertion of white Southern voters from the Democrats over the issue of civil rights in the 1960s. This desertion supplied the Republican Party with its sense of grievance, populist fervour and historical depth. Its confederate roots were apparent not only during the Republican primaries in 2000, several of which revolved around the right to fly the Confederate flag, but also during those moments in Florida when it looked as if a recount might occur. Touchiness, intransigence, paranoia over centralised authority, close relations with the military and a militaristic culture, scorn for judges, and a refusal to abide by the law if it does not go one's way, disregard for African-Americans, if not outright racism, too much power in too few hands: when have Americans seen this before, if not in the South in the years leading up to the Civil War?

> 'the struggle for Clinton in the US was for the legitimacy of the federal government itself'

Implausibly, Anderson argues that the Democrats behaved no differently than the Republicans in Florida. But the Democrats were seeking a recount, and the Republicans were blocking one. Likewise, Anderson argues that the courts were equally partisan. But while the largely-Democratic Florida Supreme Court had the constitutional responsibility for overseeing the election, the Republican-dominated US Supreme Court was explicitly forbidden from doing so by the US Constitution, which assigns the responsibility for resolving national electoral disputes to Congress. Anderson blames Gore for his own defeat because Gore did not *initially* call for a total recount. But perhaps the easiest way to refute his commensurability thesis is to imagine what the United States would have been like had Gore somehow gotten his recount and wound up as President. In contrast to the Bush presidency, of which the Democrats were originally too tolerant, a Gore Presidency would have been a four-year nightmare of complaints, investigations, lawsuits, character assassination and sour feeling: a replay of Republican behaviour during the Clinton Presidency. In casually equating the two parties, Anderson wholly misunderstands the nature of the right wing in the United States, especially its extra-legal character that descends from its Confederate (as well as its frontier) past.

It is true, of course, that the relation between the left in the United States and the Democratic Party was shaped by the imperial presidency of the Cold War, but this relation was the opposite from what Anderson describes. Ever since the war in Vietnam, the American left has *repudiated* the imperial presidency, viewing it as the tool of anti-Communist oppression and hypocrisy. Too many American leftists share Anderson's view that the American President is inevitably a force for evil and corporate greed, and that electoral politics is largely a sham. The Watergate and Iran-Contra affairs strengthened their view that the Presidency was the site of duplicity, manipulation, and abuse of power. Moreover, the essential thrust of the 1960s social movements lay in their critique of authority! From 1992 on, the extra-congressional American left was intensely anti-Clinton, often for reasons that reflected their own weakness and lack of political savvy, for example in relation to his compromise on the question of gays in the military. Lack of left support, in turn, was a contributing factor to Clinton's many compromises with the Republicans. Only with his impeachment in 1998 did the American left begin to awaken to the significance of the Presidency, the nature of the right-wing threat, and, indeed, to the importance of electoral politics itself. Anderson's article would return it to its dogmatic, apolitical slumber.

To Europeans, these matters may seem internal, family affairs, largely driven by Clinton's polarising personality. In fact, the impeachment and the election were also global events that historians will seek to understand for centuries to come. The matter that Anderson places at the centre of all contemporary politics, marketisation, was also at their centre. When Anderson reduces the impeachment and the election to juridical considerations, he shows that he does not understand the extent to which the struggle for hegemony is an ongoing social and cultural struggle.

Domestically, what lay behind the impeachment was the struggle over the public sector. Of course, this question took a different shape in the neo-liberal US than in social-democratic Europe. Whereas in Europe the left could still struggle for health, education or housing, in the US Clinton had to struggle for the legitimacy of the federal government itself. Far from smoothing out Reagan's rough edges,

Clinton rather brilliantly used Reaganite issues to build support for the government rather than to undermine it. For example, the Reaganites used the budget deficit to discredit government; Clinton showed that only the government could gain control of the deficit. The Reaganites used the issue of crime to discredit 'liberal pampering'; Clinton used the issue to support gun control.

The public sector was also at stake in the 2000 election, in which Bush kept repeating 'it's *your* surplus, not the government's'. Gore at least responded 'it's also your government'. After running an unconscionably poor campaign - losing three debates to George W. Bush! - he linked the presidential election to the struggle for the vote. In so doing he called attention to the profound fund of meanings that lies behind the federal government, in contrast to the Republicans' portrayal of government as the enemy. Throughout these events, the contours of a new, post-New Deal American majority - women, minorities and labour - could be glimpsed, albeit dimly. To miss this is to have a tin ear for American politics.

Anderson's editorial, published in the March/April issue of *New Left Review*, concludes by citing Alexander Cockburn's view that the 2000 elections had brought America 'the best of all possible worlds'. As Anderson glosses Cockburn's Panglossian view, the election delivered 'a richly merited quietus to the Clinton era, without giving undue power to Bush, while showing that Nader could indeed make all the difference'. By way of contrast, Anderson mocks the dire predictions of the unenlightened American left that a Bush Presidency would 'subvert civil rights for women and blacks, demolish worker protection, destroy the environment, mismanage the business cycle, and retreat from internationalism abroad'. The superiority of vulgar left opinion to Anderson's carefully reasoned alternative is obvious.

Anderson's failure to see that there were important political issues at stake in US politics in the last several years is linked to his unmediated approach to America's global role. Weirdly, he argues that, 'for the left, be it American or non-American, the primary criterion should in principle be the external rather than internal platforms of the candidates, since this is where what they do, as hegemonic masters of the world, always matters'. But what is Anderson's criterion for judging a foreign policy platform? He takes it for granted that *any* American intervention is wrong. Thus he criticises Gore for urging US 'military interventions' (actually Gore urged interventions *simpliciter*) 'to uphold the American values of democracy and human rights', while praising Republicans for 'restricting the grounds' for US intervention. Similarly, he concludes that 'it is a relief [that] Gore has been defeated', and that while we should not necessarily be comforted by Bush's election, 'we can say that his lack of knowledge or interest in the world outside the US is a positive sign'.

Long ago Antonio Gramsci, a major influence on Anderson's political thought, argued that anti-Americanism was the ideology of parasitic classes. The United States, he argued in 'Fordism and Americanisation', was too important, too complex, and often played too progressive a role, to justify the sneering dismissal it often evoked. One great achievement of the Clinton Presidency was to counter the one-sided anti-Americanism that began with the Fordist expansion of the 1920s, and reached its (entirely understandable) climax with the Vietnam War. Before the events of 11 September, Bush went far toward destroying Clinton's achievement, and Anderson's arguments drive toward the same end. In his view, Americans should vote for the candidate most ignorant of and least interested in foreign affairs.

The consequences of Anderson's opposition to America's global role in any capacity can be grasped by considering 'Scurrying toward Bethlehem', his recent editorial concerning the Israel/Palestine conflict. The editorial is a brilliant account of Zionism's 'dual nature': 'a movement of European ethnic nationalism' and 'a form of European overseas colonialism', and I agree with its political goals: two, strong, independent states based on the withdrawal of the Israeli settlements. I can also understand Anderson's opposition to the *content* of the Oslo accords, insofar as they reduced the Palestinian claims to isolated regions, rather than to an integral state. My disagreement is with the role he envisions for the US.

I n Anderson's view, the US's role can only be a negative and self-interested one. 'The Madrid Conference and Oslo Accords', he writes, 'were the local equivalent of the extension of NATO to Eastern Europe and the Balkan War; tying up the looser ends left by a global knockout [i.e. the Gulf War]'. Rejecting any Western attempt to broker or force a settlement, repudiating Edward Said's argument that the case for Palestine should be made in the Western countries, Anderson views a forced American withdrawal from the Middle East as the best hope for the region. Writing before 11 September, he hopes for the 'toppling' of 'Muburak's moth-eaten dictatorship in Cairo, cordially despised by the Egyptian masses', and of the 'feudal plutocracy in Riyadh [Saudi Arabia], perched above a sea of rightless immigrants'. On the one hand, we can see here Anderson's prescience in resituating the Israel/Palestine conflict in the broader Arab and Islamic context, whose importance became obvious after 11 September. On the other hand, without the involvement of the US, along with Russia and Europe, the only current replacement for the regimes in Egypt and Saudi Arabia would be the forces that bombed the World Trade Centre and the Pentagon.

The truth is that the Middle East suffered terribly from America's cold war practice of building up Islamic fundamentalism, secular despotism, and the Israeli right as bulwarks against Communism. At the same time, few things could be more dreadful to imagine than a Middle East in which the Western (including American) political and cultural presence is absent. Caught between a bullying fundamentalism that views everything modern as *Jahiliyya* (darkness) and archaic, secular despotisms, the region desperately needs a dialogue with the West, including with America's respect for difference, its demotic mass culture, and its commitment to women's rights, as well as with Europe's experience with international co-operation and social democracy. Such a dialogue will not occur without a vigorous Western political and, inevitably, military presence. While I would be more than happy to see Europe lead the way in bringing this about, for reasons I will not attempt to analyse here I do not believe that is going to happen.

Since 11 September, of course, a major US presence in the region has become inevitable. But consider how little light Anderson's approach sheds on this development. If, on the one hand, the American (and British) presence still risks sparking a fundamentalist backlash in many countries, a humanitarian disaster in Pakistan and Afghanistan, the internal collapse of Israel and the transformation of the Palestinian struggle from a national to a religious one, it has also opened up many pathways for progress: the end of Russia's isolation, the destruction of Bush's unilateralism, the strengthening of the United Nations and other international institutions, and, above all, increased voice for democratic and secular voices in the Muslim world, for example in Iran. Without question, it is still too early to predict in which direction events will move. But insofar as we can understand, and if possible, influence them, we need a more nuanced analysis of the American role, not one that is reflexively oppositional.

To conclude: as someone who has read *New Left Review* since the 1960s, I share Anderson's view that the proper starting point for understanding the present conjuncture is the transformation of capitalism that began in the 1970s. As I have suggested, however, this transformation is not reducible to the rise of neo-liberal economics. In addition, it has transfigured global power relations and local cultures in ways we have not yet begun to fathom. One obvious consequence, however, is that the United States has moved to a position of even greater centrality than that which it occupied earlier. To fail to analyse this with precision, nuance and depth is to misunderstand the world in which we live.

To be sure, the US is guilty of world-historical crimes in Vietnam, Iraq, Saudi Arabia, Indonesia, Guatemala, Cuba, Chile and elsewhere. Yet only a shallow and undialectical mind - characteristically non-Andersonian - could maintain that its role as global hegemon has always been negative, or that the left should invariably oppose the US's external activities. Any reasonable approach to understanding the US's hegemonic role would include Woodrow Wilson's understanding that the new forces of destruction required new international institutions, Franklin Roosevelt's understanding that opposition to fascism required a heightened commitment to social justice, and even certain aspects of the cold war such as the Marshall Plan, the green revolution, the economic development of parts of Asia, and the ending of apartheid. Even the Presidency of Bill Clinton, largely wrecked by Anderson's 'paper tigers', aspired toward internationalism, which it equated with globalisation. As for George W. Bush, it is still too early to know how he will be viewed.

Finally, like many Europeans, Anderson does not appreciate the way in which American culture affects its hegemonic role. America is essentially a nation of immigrants. Its identity does not reflect pride in a particular race or people, but is rather an expression of choice and, almost invariably, gratitude. While one cannot go so far as to agree with Woodrow Wilson, who called the US 'the only altruistic power', there has been a *periodic* convergence between its needs and those of the world as a whole. Certainly, the extraordinary global (including Muslim) response to the terrorist attacks of 11 September show that the world trade centre was more than the symbol of US greed, arrogance and racism that the terrorists presumably took it to be. That response has been so far marked by a remarkable process of *dereification*, symbolised by the pictures of the 'missing' found everywhere in New York, the capsule biographies in the *New York Times*, and by the statements by so many global visitors, that the trade centre was not merely - as Eduard Shevardnadze put it - American and global, but was also Georgian, Greek, Islamic, Latin, Asian, British, and European. America, in short, cannot avoid using its influence on an international scale; the only questions are with whom, how, and to what ends.

I want to thank Michael Rustin, Uri Ram and Nancy Fraser for helpful comments.

Politics of memory/states of terror

David Slater

David Slater *argues that we need to remember the history of Western invasiveness in the rest of the world if we are to address the international problems facing us now.*

In the aftermath of the events of 11 September, the geopolitical future of the world has been transformed. In that transformation the position of the United States in the world and the relations between West and non-West will become increasingly central. At the same time, what is emphasised as being crucial today will always be a reflection of the complex interweaving of a politics of memory with a politics of forgetting. The Mexican writer Carlos Fuentes recently commented in a debate on US foreign policy that the United States of Amnesia might be a more appropriate term for the USA. But to what extent is this an accurate depiction? Perhaps it might be more relevant to distinguish an official memory which recalls events such as the Declaration of Independence, Pearl Harbour, the end of the Vietnam War, from events which are customarily consigned to oblivion. Clearly, what is vital here is the struggle over what is remembered and for what purpose, and what is forgotten and why. This might relate to specific events or to the re-assertion of a particular vision. When, for example, Berlusconi underlines what he sees as the superiority of Western values, or when Francis Fukuyama declares that 'the West has won' in his end-of-history fable, an older colonial vision of world truth is being re-activated and re-fortified.[1]

What remains vital to the deployment of any geopolitical power is the construction of an ensemble of meanings, values and aspirations to legitimise that deployment. In this moment, notions of 'civilisation', 'democracy', 'freedom' and 'justice' are welded into place to justify a war against terror. That terror is immanently ascribed to the other, either as a shadowy network of 'Islamic fundamentalists' or a US-defined list of 'rogue states'.[2] 'Terror' is what is done to 'us in the West', whilst we endure in our beneficent mission of transferring our superior values and practices to the recipient non-West. To wage war against the other that dares to terrorise back is intrinsic to that mission.

Against this official backdrop, one of the ways we can respond is by critically contextualising the effects of power and the forms of terror, so that we re-activate realities that reveal another reading of global politics. In this short intervention I want to consider two examples. First, I want to refer to some key effects of the United States acting in the world - to the effects of its geopolitical interventions; and second, I want to take one or two historical dimensions of the Palestine/Israel question and relate these dimensions to the imperial role played by Britain, now the lone superpower's 'junior partner'. In both cases my aim is to problematise questions of power, terror and memory, and in so doing help to locate the antagonism towards Western dominance that is so justifiably rooted across the diverse regions of the global South.

Empire and its invasive effects

Empire became so intrinsically our American way of life that we rationalised and suppressed the nature of our means in the euphoria of our enjoyment of the ends.
W.A.Williams, *Empire as a Way of Life*, OUP 1980, p ix

I don't see why we need to stand by and watch a country go Communist due to

---

1. Francis Fukuyama, 'We Remain at the End of History', *Independent*, 11.10.01, p5; for a comment on Berlusconi, see *Guardian*, 3.10.01, p18; and for some critical remarks on the colonial connection see Rana Kabbani, *Guardian*, 9.10.01, p24.
2. For two recent texts on 'rogue states', see William Blum, *Rogue State - a guide to the world's only superpower*, Common Courage Press, Maine 2000; and Noam Chomsky, *Rogue States*, Pluto Press, London 2000.

the irresponsibility of its own people.

> Henry Kissinger, quoted in L. Schoultz, *National Security and United States Policy toward Latin America,* Princeton University Press, 1987, p284

It is never too late to remember and analyse the arrogance of power. When a New Yorker on the day after 11 September looked into the camera and exclaimed 'we are *the* Superpower: how *dare* they do this?', we were presented with one quotidian response to the reality of an invaded pride. But the antagonism towards the United States is not rooted in a posited envy of its way of life, but in an opposition to the detrimental effects of its state's global strategy of enduring invasiveness.

However, unlike the Europe of Empire and colonialism, the United States from its anti-colonial inception has always officially supported the self-determination of peoples and the struggle against European colonialism. With the exception of the Philippines, colonial annexation has never been the preference of the 'Empire of Liberty'; it has opted for the creation of protectorates, as in the cases of Cuba and Haiti; in addition regular military interventions in Central America and the Caribbean were characteristic features of US imperial power in the earlier part of the twentieth century, to be modified in the 1930s under Franklin D Roosevelt's 'Good Neighbor Policy'.[3] Rather than through territorial annexation, the geopolitical power of the United States has been rooted in its varied capacities (military, economic, political); and it has always been supported by the co-operation of the internally dominant sectors of peripheral societies, to penetrate and to re-configure the modes of governance within these societies. The illustration of these various modalities of intervention is needed not only to counter the myths of governmental narrative, but also as part of our attempt to nurture an alternative politics of memory, and another vision of terror - the terror of sanctioned power. It is possible to identify seven types of action which taken together represent a comprehensive strategy of geopolitical intervention.

1. Interventions to overturn elected governments
In contrast to the well-rehearsed argument that the West and in particular the

---

3. For a recent and thorough historical analysis of US foreign policy in the Americas, see Lars Schoultz, *Beneath the United States*, Harvard University Press, Cambridge 1999.

United States has diffused and continues to diffuse democracy to third world societies, it needs to be recalled that the United States has intervened to *terminate* democratic governments that sought to develop policies that were independent of US power. In Iran in 1953, the democratically elected government of Mossadegh, who was a conservative nationalist and a supporter of the nationalisation of the Anglo-Iranian Oil Company, was overthrown by a CIA-backed coup. The coup restored the Shah to power, initiating a twenty-five year period of severe repression, while the oil industry was restored to foreign (essentially Anglo-American) ownership.[4] Similarly, in 1954 in Guatemala, a CIA-backed coup overthrew the democratically elected government of Arbenz, who had initiated a programme of land reform which was strongly opposed by the United Fruit Company. The United States preferred the installation of a military regime to the possibility of a reforming, redistributing government acting as a possible example for other Latin American countries. The coup initiated a forty-year period of state terror, death squads, torture, disappearances and executions.[5] Other interventions which overturned democratically elected governments took place in the Dominican Republic in 1965, and Chile in 1973, for which the arrogance of US power is captured in the Kissinger quotation cited above. In the case of the Nicaraguan Revolution, the Sandinista government which had won an election in 1984, an election which was judged by independent observers to be fair and legitimate, was destabilised by the Reagan Administration and subsequently lost the 1990 elections. In the present media coverage of the 2001 elections the 1984 Sandinista victory is predominantly forgotten - erased from the record.

2. Transgressions of national sovereignty which do not represent the actual overthrow of democratically elected governments

Such transgressions took place in Cuba in 1961 (unsuccessfully), Grenada in 1983 and Panama in 1989. In the Panamanian case, the US invasion, which included the landing of 13,000 troops, was code-named 'Operation Just Cause' and its primary objectives were to 'defend democracy in Panama' and 'combat drug trafficking'. In thirteen hours, more than four hundred bombs were

---

4. See Gabriel Kolko, *Confronting the Third World*, Pantheon Books, New York 1988, pp72-77.
5. For a full account of the background to CIA operations in Guatemala, see Nick Cullather, *Secret History*, Stanford University Press, Stanford 1999.

dropped by US war planes, large areas of Panama City were burned to the ground and over 10,000 people were left homeless. In the end the Panamanian leader General Manuel Noriega, a previous CIA agent, was arrested and sentenced by a court in Miami to forty years in prison for conspiring to smuggle drugs into the United States. In the case of Grenada, conflicts within the radical New Jewel Movement regime, which culminated in the murder of Maurice Bishop, plus the presence of a small number of Cuban construction workers, provided a pretext for US intervention and the landing of 6000 marines. The Reagan Administration justified its invasion in relation to article 6 of the Rio Pact of 1947 which, it claimed, legitimises intervention when regional security is threatened by an extra-continental conflict or any other situation that might endanger the peace of America. The United States acted unilaterally in accordance with its own strategic imperatives, and failed to convene a meeting of the Organisation of American States as was required by article 6 of the Rio Treaty. As one author put it: 'the invasion ... was meant to set an example to those who were deemed to threaten the national security of the United States'.[6]

3. Support for dictatorships

The termination of independent democratic government and the transgression of national sovereignty has its reverse side - a historical record of support for pro-Western dictatorships. In South America, military regimes in Argentina, Brazil, Chile and Uruguay were not destabilised and undermined but supported.[7] In Africa, the repressive political and social order Mobutu imposed on Zaire was possible only due to loyal American support for him after 1965. In Angola, the United States together with South Africa did everything feasible to undermine the legitimate MPLA government from 1975 onwards and continued to support UNITA's war of destabilisation with appalling results for the future of peace and security for the Angolan people.[8] In Indonesia not only is it necessary to recall the role played by the United States in supporting the post-1965 Suharto military

---

6. See Frank Niess, *A Hemisphere to Itself*, Zed Books, London 1990.
7. For example, in the case of the 1964 military coup in Brazil, the United States provided up to $1.5 billion in financial support during the regime's first four years - see *Confronting the Third World*, p159 (full ref note 4).
8. See Victoria Brittain, *Death of Dignity*, Pluto Press, London 1998.

regime but also its nefarious part in the 'final solution' to Indonesia's Communist problem. Estimates vary as to the numbers massacred - one CIA estimate was of 250,000 deaths, in a Communist party (the PKI) of 3 million members - and the CIA itself classified the slaughter of Communists in Indonesia as 'one of the worst mass murders of the 20th century'.[9] These are examples which stand out as being particularly significant in their long-term geopolitical impact, but there have been many more, as the history of the Middle East testifies. The key point here is to re-assert the historical record and perhaps recall what Edward Said wrote some years ago - that 'rarely before in human history has there been so massive an intervention of force and ideas from one culture to another as there is today from America to the rest of the world'.[10]

4. Assassinations

A more targeted form of intervention, often unrecorded, is the CIA policy of assassinations, which was made illegal in 1976, only to be re-activated by President Bush in the wake of 11 September. In 1975 a Senate Committee, in its report on alleged assassinations, wrote that it did not believe that the acts of assassination it had examined represented the 'real American character'; rather they were 'aberrations'. However, as William Blum shows (for reference see note 2), from the early 1950s to the mid-1970s there were over 40 recorded incidents of assassination plots, largely aimed at third world leaders. In the single case of Fidel Castro, official US records published in July 1997 showed that the CIA launched at least eight attempts on the Cuban leader's life in the 1960s, including attempted shootings and bombings, lethal pills and on one notorious occasion an exploding cigar (*Guardian*, 1.11.97). Nor should we assume that political leaders were the only targets, as was clearly shown during the Vietnam War with the launch in the early 1970s of 'Operation Phoenix' which would 'neutralise' - arrest or kill - suspected Vietcong supporters in South Vietnam. Innocent villagers were systematically arrested, tortured or killed.[11]

---

9. Quoted in Noam Chomsky, *Powers and Prospects*, Pluto Press, London 1996 p195.
10. Edward Said, *Culture and Imperialism*, Chatto & Windus, London 1993, p387. On the Middle East see *Confronting the Third World* pp9-91; and Joe Stork, 'Oil, Islam and Israel: US policy and Democratic Change in the Middle East', in Jochen Hippler (ed), *The Democratisation of Disempowerment*, Pluto Press, London 1995, pp153-172.
11. See Robert Buzzanco, *Vietnam and the Transformation of American Life*, Blackwell, Oxford 1999, p103.

5. Disregard for international public law

The policy of assassination can be interpreted within the wider framework of this disregard. The more than forty-year blockade of Cuba stands as one example. This strategy has been condemned by the UN, the European Union, and the Inter-American Juridical Committee, which has ruled that such a series of measures as the trade embargo against Cuba violates international law (see Chomsky's *Rogue States*, p2). As a second example, in the case of US support for the *contras* in Nicaragua during the 1980s, the International Court in The Hague found the United States guilty of violating both international law and its treaty obligations to Nicaragua, and ordered Washington to stop the intervention and negotiate a reparations settlement with Nicaragua. After winning the 1990 elections, the US-backed government of President Chamorro, under pressure from Washington, withdrew the lawsuit, the costs of which had risen to $17 billion, and subsequently Washington forgave $260 million in loans to Nicaragua.[12] Other examples of a disregard for international law are reflected in the use of American-defined powers of extra-territorial jurisdiction (as for example with the case of Noriega) and in a reluctance to abide by international treaty obligations.[13]

6. Acts of international terror

Not only can we point to a certain disregard for international jurisdiction but more seriously to acts of international terror. The bombing of Libya in 1986, the shooting down of an Iranian passenger plane in 1988, the joint US/UK bombing of Iraq after the Gulf War and the bombing of Sudan and Afghanistan in 1998 are examples of the unlawful acts of the world's most powerful rogue state. But these acts are officially described as 'retaliation' for acts of terror presumed to have been committed by other countries or networks, and often Article 51 of the UN Charter is creatively interpreted to recast acts of state violence as legitimate measures taken in the exercise of the right of self-defence.[14]

---

12. See Robert H Holden and Eric Zolov (eds), *Latin America and the United States: a documentary history*, Oxford University Press, New York and Oxford 2000, pp300-301.
13. As argued in the *American Journal of International Law*, 92, 1998, and quoted in Chomsky's *Rogue States*, p216 (full ref note 2).
14. Article 51 of the UN Charter is also referred to in Article 5 of the NATO Treaty, which stipulates that an armed attack against one or more of the parties to the treaty shall be considered an 'attack against them all', and that if such an attack occurs action can be taken, including the use of armed force, to restore and maintain the security of the North Atlantic area - see www.nato.int/docu/basictxt/treaty.htm‡ Art05.

7. The SOA

Within the United States itself, it is important to remember the activities of the US Army School of the Americas (SOA). This School was moved from Panama in 1984 to Fort Benning, Georgia, and by 1996 it had trained approximately 60,000 Latin American military and police personnel. Seven US Army training manuals used by the School between 1989 and 1991 were declassified in 1996. The manuals provided instruction on the detection and suppression of anti-government political and military activities, and contained information indicating how the US Army trained Latin American military and police officers in a variety of interrogation techniques. As has been noted SOA graduates have led a number of military coups in Latin America, and as Blum suggests, it is unlikely that the full scope of atrocities committed by the School's graduates will ever be known.[15] What has been documented is evidence of the training by the US Army of Latin American military and police personnel in the skills of institutionalised terror.

These seven facets of geopolitical intervention do not provide a complete guide but they do point to an alternative reality to the official discourse surrounding America's role in the world, past and present. They also suggest another reservoir of memory which can be used to think through other states of terror, often forgotten in a silencing of the past. The modes of intervention outlined above also draw us to the invasive effects of imperial power and to the roots of so much anger at so much injustice.

Let us now turn to another and central issue in explaining the roots of antagonism towards the West, and especially in the Arab world - the question of Palestine. In this case I want to briefly look at the historical role played by the 'junior partner' of the world's lone superpower, but at a time when Britain was itself an imperial player on the world stage.

The West and the question of Palestine - geopolitical origins of an injustice

The tragedy in Palestine is not just a local one; it is a tragedy for the world, because it is an injustice that is a menace to the world's peace.

Arnold Toynbee, 1968, quoted in the UN Report on Palestine 1990

---

15. See Blum's *Rogue State*, pp62-63 (full ref note 2); and Holden and Zolov's *Latin America and the United States* pp313-316 (full ref note 12).

On 2 November 1917 the British Foreign Secretary Arthur James Balfour wrote to Lord Rothschild and conveyed a declaration of sympathy with Jewish Zionist aspirations. The Balfour Declaration, which was later to be included in the League of Nations mandate for Palestine, was a short statement of 67 words, but its impact was to be profound and lasting. In re-examining the declaration, it is worthwhile remembering the following: first that the British government 'favoured the establishment in Palestine of a national home for the Jewish people'; and second 'that nothing shall be done which may prejudice the civil and religious rights of existing non-Jewish communities in Palestine', or equally the 'rights and political status enjoyed by Jews in any other country'.[16]

What I think is important to underline here is the reference made to the '*civic* and *religious* rights of the non-Jewish communities' rather than to their *political* rights, which contrasts with the 'rights and *political status*' associated with the Jewish people. Moreover, the Palestinians and Arab peoples are not written into the declaration as such but are referred to as the 'non-Jewish communities in Palestine'. In other words, their identity as well as their political rights to self-determination as a people are not explicitly recognised. In addition, and in a revealing memo written two years later to Lord Curzon, Balfour asserted that the Allies did not propose to even consult the 'wishes of the present inhabitants of Palestine', thus contravening Article 22 of the League of Nations Covenant. This was explained by the fact that the powers of the day were committed to Zionism, 'be it right or wrong', since 'it is rooted in age-long traditions' and 'of far profounder import than the desires and prejudices of the 700,000 Arabs who now inhabit that ancient land' (*Origins* pp25-6). Perhaps the only positive aspect of this statement was that it did at least include the recognition of the existence of 700,000 Palestinian and Arab people in the land of Palestine at that time. In contrast, one of the founding slogans of the Zionist Organisation was 'a land with no people for people without land', i.e. the Palestinian and Arab peoples were erased from the map of Palestine so as to help legitimise the creation of a homeland for the Jewish people. Clearly, however, Balfour's candidly expressed views on the posited insignificance of the 'desires and prejudices' of 700,000 Arabs captured a form of Western prejudice that has cast a long and enduring shadow over the Middle East region.[17]

---

16. See The United Nations, *The Origins and Evolution of the Palestine Problem 1917-1988*, New York 1990, p8. Hereinafter this is referred to in the text as *Origins*.
17. For the now classic study of Orientalist visions of the Middle East, see Edward Said's *Orientalism*, Penguin Books 1978.

Britain's League of Nations mandate over Palestine came into force in 1923 and in the period up to the Second World War, the land of Palestine witnessed a continual and sizeable immigration of Jewish settlers, especially from Germany during the rise of Nazi terror. By 1939 the Jewish population in Palestine numbered over 445,000 out of a total of about 1,500,000 - nearly 30 per cent compared to the less than 10 per cent twenty years before. Similarly, by the end of 1939, Jewish holdings of land had risen almost threefold since the start of the Mandate (see *Origins* pp72, 42). Arnold Toynbee, the eminent historian who had dealt directly with the Palestine Mandate in the British Foreign Office, wrote in 1968 that if Palestine had remained under Ottoman Turkish rule, or if it had become an independent Arab state in 1918, Jewish immigrants would not have been admitted into Palestine in such large numbers. Toynbee went on to comment that, 'the reason why the State of Israel exists today and why today 1,500,000 Palestinian Arabs are refugees is that, for 30 years, Jewish immigration was imposed on the Palestinian Arabs by British military power until the immigrants were sufficiently numerous and sufficiently well-armed to be able to fend for themselves with tanks and planes of their own'. He concluded with the prescient observation, quoted above, that the Palestinian tragedy is not a local matter but a question for the world since its injustice is a threat to world peace.

Britain terminated its mandate over Palestine in 1948, several months before the time envisaged in the United Nations plan. As is known the creation of the State of Israel was preceded by a wave of terror against the Palestinian Arab population. The 1990 United Nations Report on Palestine concluded that the terror spread among the Palestinian population was a crucial factor for future political developments since it led to a mass exodus of refugees into neighbouring countries. The number of Palestinian refugees resulting from the hostilities was estimated to number 726,000 by the end of 1949 - half the indigenous population of Palestine (*Origins* p135). The declaration establishing the State of Israel made reference to the right of the Jewish people to a 'national rebirth in its own country', a right it was noted that had been recognised in the Balfour Declaration and reaffirmed in the Mandate of the League of Nations. That claimed right went together with the expulsion of Palestinians from their homeland and the beginnings of a process of territorial expansionism; here the twin origins of the word territory - i.e. land and terror - were brought together.

The territorial expansionism of the Israeli state has been reflected in the 1967

43

war, the invasion of South Lebanon in 1982 (with an estimated 17,000 civilian deaths) and the continuing establishment of new and illegal Jewish settlements in occupied Palestinian land. UN Resolution 242 of November 1967, which was adopted by the Security Council, stipulated the 'inadmissibility of the acquisition of territory by war' and called for a 'just settlement of the refugee problem'. But this resolution and many other UN resolutions have been defied by Israel - to whom the United States has given unwavering support. Since the end of the Second World War, Israel has been and remains, for the West and especially the United States, a key 'strategic asset' in the geopolitical heartland of the Middle East.

Resistance to Israeli occupation in the first and second *intifadas* has been met by Israeli state violence. In the period 1988 to 1994 Israel interrogated on average five thousand Palestinians per year. According to official statistics, of the 83,321 Palestinians tried in military courts in the West Bank and Gaza Strip between 1988 and 1993 only 3.2 per cent were acquitted. A majority of interrogation subjects were subjected to severe beatings, many of which involved broken bones and hospitalisation. These methods were subsequently reviewed and changed into a package of measures that included beatings that left no marks, painful body positioning and sensory disorientation.[18] But there have of course been other effects. For example, one year into the second intifada starting in 2000, 706 Palestinians have been killed (about four times the number of Israeli deaths), with 30 per cent being children; 16,204 have been injured; 809 Palestinian homes have been demolished by Israeli authorities; 112,900 olive trees have been uprooted from Palestinian land and as a result of Israeli closures there has been an estimated shortfall in Palestinian GNP of $1.5 billion from September 2000 to March 2001.[19]

Finally, as Edward Said writes, 'equipped with the latest in American-donated fighter-bombers, helicopter gunships, tanks and missiles ... Israel has been grinding down a dispossessed people without ... any of the protective institutions of a modern state'. Israel's cruel confinement of 1.3 million people in the Gaza strip and of nearly two million in the West Bank has 'few parallels in the annals of colonialism'. Even under apartheid, as Said reminds the reader, F-16 jets were never used to bomb African homelands, as they are now being sent against

---

18. For these statistics based on Human Rights Watch information see James Ron, 'Varying Methods of State Violence', *International Organization*, 51, 2, Spring 1997, pp275-276.
19. The information is from a variety of sources including the World Bank, the UN and the Palestine Red Crescent Society - see *Palestine News*, October-December London 2001, p4.

Palestinian towns and villages.[20]

Thinking about the geopolitical origins of injustice and the connections between the politics of memory and states of terror, I came across the following report which struck me as germane to the notes I have outlined above, acting as a fitting coda.

When Tony Blair recently visited Gaza, a *Guardian* reporter came across a 65-year resident of the refugee camp known as 'Beach Camp' because of its proximity to the Mediterranean seashore: "'What more does Blair want from us?" asked the 65-year old Ahmad, putting down the pipe he was smoking to emphasise his dismay, "It's because of his predecessor, Balfour, that we live like this today'" (*Guardian*, 2.11.01). It would be difficult to find a more poignant example of the significance of a politics of memory rooted in such a deep and legitimate sense of injustice.

Invasive power and the rising tide of fury

In contemporary Washington, belligerence and bellicosity are the order of the day. The devastating attacks on the symbols of America's financial and military power have unleashed a new force for vengeance and a desire for an unending war on terror . In a world where one power is globally pre-eminent - Bill Clinton's 'indispensable nation', a nation that has believed since the nineteenth century in its 'manifest destiny' to take its purportedly superior way of life to all corners of the globe - there are also other worlds, of the dispossessed, the disrespected and the colonised. (And of course, inside 'America', as elsewhere, there are worlds inhabited by citizens who believe in global justice, equality and respect for difference, cultural and political.) The long-term effects of the invasive power of the Occident, and especially of the 'colossus of the North', have been to open up a sea of antagonism within which many currents ebb and flow. Acts of terror need to be treated as criminal acts to be responded to within the parameters of international law and justice, rather than being elevated into acts of war. The geopolitical impact of 11 September 2001 may be taken as a moment to rethink a wider range of intersections among power, terror and memory. In re-examining the illegitimacy and historical duplicity of invasive power, and calling for action to redress the injustices past and present of such invasiveness, we can more effectively keep open the crucial pathways for cross-cultural dialogue and critical understanding. In the world in which we all move, such pathways are needed more urgently than ever before.

20. Edward Said, 'A People in Need of Leadership', *New Left Review*, 11, September/ October 2001, pp27-28.

Covering (up) the 'war on terrorism'

The master frame and the media chill

Bob Hackett

Bob Hackett offers a Canadian perspective on press responses to 11 September.

Two weekends after the 11 September atrocity, I watched with appreciation the respected American journalist and media critic James Fallows. He was warning his colleagues that in the attack's emotional aftermath independent journalism was at risk of being swallowed by patriotism. Just one problem: Fallows was speaking not on an American network, but on Canada's main public broadcaster, the CBC. In Canada, there has been some semblance of debate over fundamental issues, even inspiration and intellectual courage. No one person could track the ocean of coverage, but here are some of the moments I appreciated: on CBC Radio on September 11, a philosophy professor cautioning against the metaphors of Pearl Harbour and war - analogies which imply total mobilisation, martial obedience, and much else; Neil MacDonald, also on CBC, questioning the definition of 'terrorism', which each state defines differently according to its own perceived interests; CBC television's CounterSpin and Town Hall programmes, and Rex

Murphy on radio, accessing Muslim Canadians and other often marginalised voices and viewpoints; Jonathan Manthorpe in the *Vancouver Sun*, describing how 'meddling by western powers' had 'fuelled the radicalization of the Middle East'.

At the same time, Canadian journalism is not immune to the silencing pressures on American media - through the shared trauma of 11 September, close personal and social ties, the influence of American media on Canadian popular culture, and our partial dependence on US-based networks and wire services for foreign news. And in the US, voices of dissent and caution have been marginalised, even censored.

As the Bush administration's rhetoric escalated rapidly, from 'there has been a terrorist attack' to 'an act of war' to 'we are at war', the media's dominant narratives, the shared mindset underlying the selection and presentation of news, quickly gelled into a kind of Master Frame: This is a war (not a campaign or police action) between absolute good and absolute evil. Like a lightning bolt from Satan, 11 September was an unprovoked attack on Freedom and Democracy. You are either for us, or against us. The American people will unite behind its leaders, use whatever means and make whatever sacrifices are necessary, to crush evil and ensure the triumph of good. This is about 'Infinite Justice' - the original brand name of the retaliatory operation.

Frames are unavoidable in journalism, as in any form of effective story-telling. Comprising mostly implicit assumptions about values and reality, they help to construct coherent narratives out of a potential infinity of occurrences and information. The problem is that when they are accepted uncritically, frames can lead journalism to exclude information which, from another perspective, would be considered relevant. In America's alternative press, but rarely in the dominant media, other frames were in play - that violence begets violence, or that the double standards and hegemonism of the US government's foreign policy were part of a broader pattern from which the evil acts of 11 September emerged.

Obviously, nothing whatsoever can justify the terror attacks. It ought to go equally without saying, however, that the mass slaughter of innocent civilians in retaliation is not morally acceptable. Yet, ensconced safely within the master frame, some of America's highest-profile media pundits called for just that, including the use of nuclear weapons. A Rogue's Gallery of bloodthirsty quotes ('as for cities or countries that host these worms, bomb them into basketball courts') was posted by the New York-based media monitoring group Fairness and Accuracy in Reporting (www.fair.org) on 17 September. Perhaps these hot-headed pundits were reflecting the rage of the moment, and their own job of provocation. What is more disquieting is the way in which this Frame has continued to shape the agenda of news reporting.

Topics which fit the frame are highlighted. For example, besides the endlessly repeated visuals of planes smashing into the Towers, journalists (sometimes insensitively, sometimes courageously) told tales of human tragedy and heroism in Manhattan. And understandably so; 11 September was a made-for-TV atrocity, arousing unparalleled emotions, and offering the human interest, drama, threat and visuals at which TV excels. But beyond a certain point, the round-the-clock rescue coverage became an alibi for not exploring other topics.

Second, just as previous tyrants (Manuel Noriega, Saddam Hussein, Slobodan Milosevic) popped out of obscurity to become media villains of the month prior to previous US-led interventions, Osama bin Laden and the Taliban regime appeared everywhere. Though initially and responsibly cautious about attributing blame - mindful of the haste with which Middle Eastern extremists were fingered for the Oklahoma City bombing before it turned out to be the work of home-grown right-wing fanatics - the media soon scrambled to spotlight the Taliban's appalling human rights record - six years after it had seized power. In an unwitting indictment of its own journalism, CNN promo'd one of its documentaries as 'a side of Afghanistan you have never seen before'. In American media, the demonization of foreign villains is selective; by and large, only those who threaten US interests are newsworthy.

Not that these topics were inappropriate. The real problem is the omission of stories that do not fit the master frame. 'Silence, rigorously selective, pervades the media coverage', wrote Norman Solomon, whose column is carried in about 15 of America's smaller dailies. 'For policy-makers in Washington, the practical utility of that silence is enormous. In response to the mass murder committed by hijackers, the righteousness of US military action is clear - as long as double standards go unmentioned'.

Borrowing from American media-monitoring and alternative media web sites (e.g. mediachannel.org, fair.org, alternet.org, znet.org), here is my list of the 'top ten' questions undercovered by the dominant US media:

Why did this atrocity happen?

As former ABC producer Danny Schechter put it, 'There is all too little media reflection on how this attack connects to other things happening in the world. Was it simply aimed, as some officials have been saying, at our culture and way of life or are there specific political factors?'

Squeamishness about this question is understandable; it could wrongly be taken to imply that there is some conceivable moral justification for the atrocities. Still, beyond the identity and motives of the hijackers and their backers, US television news has shown remarkably little curiosity about the geopolitical fires which fuel fanaticism and terrorism - not just anti-liberal or anti-modernist tendencies in the Islamic world, but also (as Vancouver political scientist Peter Prontzos says), those of 'Washington's own actions, especially in the Middle East, which contribute to widespread anti-Americanism in many parts of the world'. Few North Americans know much of such actions, but independent journalists like Robert Fisk and John Pilger have covered dozens of them - from the deaths of hundreds of thousands of Iraqis in the Gulf War and in the sanctions afterwards, to the August 1998 cruise missile attack on a Sudanese pharmaceutical factory (wrongly suspected as a bin Laden depot), which killed unknown numbers of workers.

What are the policy options in response to the attack?

From the very beginning, only a unilateral military response was on the media's table. The parade of strategic analysts, 'security' experts and former government officials on American network TV defined the issue from the start, and the near total absence of debate in Congress sealed the deal. Even so, Jeff Cohen of the media monitoring group Fair argues, 'It's appalling how little mainstream media have discussed relying on the rule of law - international law - to pursue the foreign terrorists'. Multilateral action organised through the United Nations, with military action well down the priority list, an approach favoured by Canada's New Democratic Party, was ignored or contemptuously dismissed by American media pundits.

Was September 11 a case of 'blowback'?

To what extent were bin Laden's network and the Taliban regime itself made possible in part by previous US funding and training (channelled through the Pakistani security service) for the Afghan resistance to the Soviet invaders in the 1980s? Why did the US government provide $43 million to the Taliban, as part of its drug war, only months prior to the attack? More broadly, what are the implications of the huge international trade in armaments (63 per cent of it from the US in 1997), with much of it flowing to repressive regimes in the Middle East? What lessons should be drawn for future security and foreign policy?

Who is the enemy? How far do the intended targets extend? What counts as a victory?

And especially, if this is a 'war against terrorism' (as distinct from an internationally co-ordinated police action to bring a specific group of criminals to justice), then what exactly qualifies as 'terrorism'?

'American news outlets routinely define terrorism the same way that US government officials do', argues Norman Solomon. 'Sadly, the even-handed use of the label would mean sometimes affixing it directly on the US government.' The American satirist and film producer Michael Moore (who has been frozen out of US TV newscasts since 11 September) cites as one example the US backing for the Nicaraguan contras, who killed some 30,000 civilians in the 1980s.

What is the state of public opinion, not only in the US, but elsewhere in the world?

While peace rallies and public doubts at home were arguably scanted, the media were not inaccurate in reporting great support for Bush's military escalation. But they ignored polls (e.g. Reuters, 21 September) suggesting that huge majorities in Europe, Latin America and elsewhere favoured extraditing and trying the terrorists, rather than bombing their base countries.

Was September 11 really 'Islamic' terrorism? Or would it more correct to describe it, with Christopher Hitchens, as 'fascism with an Islamic face'?

Here, the coverage has been ambivalent, and probably subject to contradictory pressures. On the one hand, the Bush administration was working hard to build a coalition of 'moderate' Arab states. 'This is not a war against Islam' is a coalition mantra, and to its credit, Bush officials have distinguished between terrorism and the legitimate Islamic faith. On the other hand, the simplistic story lines of commercial TV news demand visible villains. The screens were filled with 'dancing Palestinians' and angry crowds in Pakistan. According to an e-mail from a network field assistant in Egypt, Western correspondents are not interested in the voices of sympathetic or moderate Muslims. They parachute in with pre-conceived story lines, and demand interviews with photogenically raging radicals.

What kind of political agendas are piggybacking on the tragedy? Put more bluntly, 'who benefits' in the US, the Islamic world, or elsewhere?

'How has the national security state's agenda been accelerated, how has their budget been expanded, and what corporations have seen stock value increase after the tragedy?' asks Peter Phillips, director of Project Censored, which annually identifies major stories missed by America's corporate media.

How are our civil rights being threatened?

Phillips fears that Congress's proposed anti-terrorism legislation, largely ignored by the three major networks' nightly newscasts, would contradict the Bill of Rights, and also the guarantees in the Universal Declaration of Human Rights of the right to life, liberty and security of person, and to a fair and public hearing in criminal cases. Already, hundreds of immigrants are being detained without having committed any crime, according to the School of the Americas Watch.

Is George W. Bush the legitimate commander-in-chief?

This may seem a peculiar question; legally, the US Supreme Court settled Bush's contested election months ago. But media doubts remained, and a consortium of major US news organisations launched a massive count of 180,000 Florida ballots last January. The results were scheduled for public release on 24 September - but according to Seth Mnookin (www.inside.com), they are on hold indefinitely. Said a journalist with the project (quoted anonymously), 'There's a sense that now is not the time to be writing about something that might make it look like someone else should have been elected president.'

Why is there so little talk about the war itself?

After the Gulf War, it became clear that the Patriot missiles were not as accurate as we had been told, most of the bombs weren't 'smart', and the Kuwaiti babies torn from incubators by Iraqi troops were inventions of a public relations firm. This time, without even carefully shepherded 'pools' of reporters in the combat zone, journalists may be even more dependent on Pentagon spoon-feeding and less willing to challenge official information. We can expect to hear much about the coalition's military prowess, and as little about 'collateral damage', as the Pentagon can get away with.

And the list of under-covered, outside-the-frame stories could be expanded - hate crimes (never labelled 'terrorism') against Arab-Americans, for instance.

Why have American mainstream media been so ready to abandon their once-cherished democratic role as a critical watchdog on powerholders? There is no single explanation. Journalists as well as their audiences are tempted to 'rally round the flag' in a time of national crisis, and the political and military leadership on which the media depend as a funnel for information is not about to encourage critical questioning. The 11 September events themselves made for an emotionally compelling and gut-wrenching (but in the long run, dangerously simplistic) story line built around the stuff of legend - heroes, villains and victims. Schooled in the foundational myths of nationhood, America as the world's beacon of Freedom, most TV viewers would not see the master frame as a narrative at all, but simply as 'the way things are'.

Media corporations themselves have contributed to the current narrowing of public discourse. Drastic cutbacks in international news coverage by US media, in response to corporate demands for larger profits, and to fragmented audiences, have hardly cultivated an informed citizenry. 'Having decided that readers and viewers in post-Cold War America cared more about celebrities, scandals and local news', writes David Shaw of the *LA Times*, 'news executives have reduced the space and time devoted to foreign coverage by 70% to 80% during the past 15 to 20 years'. As a result, 'the rest of the world knows far more about America than we know about ourselves, let alone what we know about them', laments Nina Burleigh, who as a *Time* reporter was one of the first American journalists to enter Iraq after the Gulf War. 'And this triumph of ignorance means that Americans can't even comprehend what motivates those who hate us.'

As media corporations converge and commercialise, they develop a corporate culture increasingly hostile to the public service ethos associated with Walter Cronkite and his generation. Years of flak from conservatives, convinced despite all the contrary evidence that the media contributed to defeat in Vietnam, have left the press anxious to prove its patriotism. Contrast Cronkite's legendary speech on TV, that the Vietnam war was not winnable, with Dan Rather's pledge on the David Letterman show: 'George Bush is the President ... Wherever he wants me to line up, just tell me where'.

And as a trump card, there's always de facto censorship. After readers complained, two columnists, one in Texas and one in Oregon, were fired for questioning Bush's courage as he 'skedaddled' from one base to another on 11 September. A similar comment about cowardice and Cruise missiles landed Politically Incorrect host Bill Maher in career-threatening hot water until he apologised. Even Ann Coulter, on the far right, lost a column at Online National Review. In a country with fewer and fewer media employers, it doesn't take too many such examples for journalists everywhere to feel the chill.

John MacArthur, publisher of *Harper's Magazine* and author of a book on censorship in the Gulf War, makes a depressing observation: 'There isn't even the spirit any more that there was in Vietnam, of scepticism, and the sense that the patriotic thing to do is to tell the American people the truth and to try to be impartial and not to be the cat's paw of the government. But when I say this on TV the reaction is overwhelming, there is tremendous hostility to the free press in this country.'

Tremendous hostility to the free press - a stunning conclusion from a country gearing up to defeat the enemies of freedom.

This article is a slightly edited version of one to be carried in a forthcoming issue of MEDIA magazine, which is published by the Canadian Association of Journalists (caj@igs.net).

Thinking ahead

The new politics of knowledge

Jonathan Rutherford

Knowledge is increasingly becoming a commodity, with trade in intellectual property rights and other forms of knowledge lying at the heart of current forms of capitalist accumulation. Can we protect the intellectual commons and create a commonwealth of knowledge?

I strongly believe that the knowledge economy is our best route for success and prosperity.

Tony Blair, 2000[1]

The communication of information and the creation of knowledge have been central to economic development since the scholasticism of mediaeval times. In the late eighteenth and nineteenth centuries, the waves of the Industrial Revolution depended upon technological and scientific innovation. During the Second World War, the invention of the programmable computer and the transistor created the conditions for a new age of information, which became manifest in the 1970s. During this decade information and communications technologies (ICTs) began to revolutionise the generation, processing and transmission of information, turning it into a fundamental source of productivity.

1.   Speech given at the DTI's '"Knowledge 2000" Conference on the Knowledge Driven Economy' at the New Connaught Rooms, London, 7.3.00, www.dti.gov.uk

54

The Centre for Educational Research and Innovation at the OECD describes member countries as facing 'a transformation of a magnitude comparable to the one of the industrial revolution.'[2] David Potter, in his Millennium Seminar at 10 Downing Street, proposed that we are 'living through a new iron age; a revolution as profound as the agrarian revolution; a new industrial revolution.'[3] Manuel Castells is emphatic about its historical significance: 'I think that, as with the industrial revolutions, there will be several information technology revolutions, of which the one constituted in the 1970s is only the first.'[4]

Sceptics counter that the internet is fundamentally no more than a delivery system that cannot compare to the revolutionary inventions of the printing press, the steam engine and electricity.[5] The precipitous collapse in the capital valuation of dotcoms and new technology companies in 2000 added weight to the argument that the 'new economy' was wishful conjecture. Colossal sums of money were lost as speculative gambles went disastrously wrong. Telecoms corporations like BT plunged into debt after frenetic bouts of acquisitions. JP Morgan Partners alone - the venture capital wing of the US investment bank - wrote off $1bn in technology investments. Alongside the greed and irrationality of the market, the downturn is symptomatic of too much investment too soon, and the initial embedding of the new technologies in often traditional modes of production. The left must take seriously the idea that a qualitatively new type of informational, knowledge driven economy is emerging, whose consequences are still largely in the future. The OECD working party on the Information Economy admitted in its 1999 report, 'we are not really certain where we are heading with all this.'[6]

2. *Draft Issues Paper: Knowledge Management in the Public and Private Sectors: Similarities and Differences in the Challenges Created by the Knowledge-Intensive Economy*, Centre for Educational Research and Innovation (CERI) and the Public Management Service (PUMA) of the OECD, 2000, www.oecd.org/puma.
3. David Potter, *Wealth Creation in the Knowledge Economy of the Next Millennium*, 27.5.99, www.number-10.gov.uk/.
4. Manuel Castells, *The Rise of the Network Society*, Blackwell 2000, p6.
5. Robert J. Gordon, *Does the 'New Economy' Measure Up to the Great Inventions of the Past?*, National Bureau of Economic Research Working Paper No. W7833, August 2000, www.nber.org; see also Adair Turner, *Just Capital - The Liberal Economy*, Macmillan 2001.
6. *Working Party on the Information Economy, OECD Workshops on the Economics of the Information Society: A Synthesis of Policy Implications* (DSTI/ICCP/IE(99)1/FINAL), 1999, www.oecd.org/.

The knowledge economy

In 1998, the World Bank Development Plan declared that, 'For countries in the vanguard of the world economy, the balance between knowledge and resources has shifted so far toward the former that knowledge has become perhaps the most important factor determining the standard of living.'[7] The US economist Robert Reich has argued that 20 per cent of the US workforce earns a living by symbolic analysis, by which he means the evaluation, analysis and codification of information, the manipulation of cultural and symbolic meaning and visual representation, and the creation of new knowledge.[8] These activities are the intangible asset of wealth creation in today's globalised economy. The utilisation of knowledge and information provides, in large part, the key competitive advantage of a company, and it is embedded in all economic sectors. Information technologies have begun to transform traditional manufacturing and distribution systems, but they have also created new types of firms, products and markets.

In 1984, the top ten largest firms by value, quoted on the London Stock Exchange, were the oil companies BP and Shell; the industrial companies GEC, ICI, BAT and BTR; a retailer, Marks and Spencer, and two pharmaceutical firms, Glaxo and Beecham. In 2001 the oil companies retain their positions, and are joined by four banks, Barclays, HSBC, the Royal Bank of Scotland and Lloyds-TSB. The industrial companies have been replaced by a new type of knowledge company, utilising intellectual property, ICTs and franchise, represented by GlaxoSmithKline, AstraZeneca, Vodaphone and BT. Like Microsoft, Cisco and Disney in the US, they are valued by their intellectual property rights and knowledge content. Banks, their profit margins for financial services increasingly cut, earn revenue by selling information. The market value of the new knowledge corporations bears no relation to their capital stock, but is derived from their ownership of software, technological know-how, information, and knowledge of the market. Ownership of specific intellectual property provides them with a monopoly position in the market. The high cost of initial research and uncertain market outcomes prohibits the entry of new firms competing on price. Competition in the knowledge economy is based on new systems and products that leave the market leader's organisation and product outdated or obsolete.

---

7. Cited in the White Paper, *Our Competitive Future: Building the Knowledge Driven Economy*, para.1.2, 1998, www.dti.gov.uk.
8. Robert Reich, *The Work of Nations*, Random House, 1999.

This monopolistic style of competition has been described by the economist Joseph Schumpeter as 'a method of economic change' which can never be stationary.[9] Capitalism, he argues, is not concerned with administering existing structures but with creating and destroying them, constantly revolutionising itself from within in a process of 'creative destruction'. Its survival is dependent upon enterprise propelling technological progress. The source of its dynamism lies in a culture of continuous innovation, and the Nietzschean figure of the entrepreneur with his 'dream to found a private kingdom'.

The new-style manufactureless or 'weightless' knowledge corporations are transforming the capitalist mode of production and consumption. In the knowledge-driven economy, the chain linking knowledge-creation, machinery and manufacturing goods for consumption is disappearing, as consumers and knowledge producers interact directly.[10] Thus branding can be seen as an attempt to manage the complex system of information-feedback loops between producers and consumers. Brands provide an emotional, even moral, appeal, which establishes a community of interest amongst customers centred around an identification with a product. Increasingly, businesses must account for the environmental and social outcomes of their goods. The extension of the production process beyond output, into the realm of sensation, imagination and symbolic capital, is redefining the economic sphere. The new corporations are organised around the production of expressive meaning. Companies like Nike and Gap trade as much on cultural meaning as they do on their physical products. Value no longer simply resides in the product or the technology, but in the ideas and symbols invested in them, and the ways these are effectively communicated to the market. Nokia mobile phones, for example, succeeded where Ericsson failed in its handset business, because Nokia designed covetable and beautiful products.

The gap between output and outcome has become a key determinant of productivity, change and the increased effectiveness of an organisation. To be successful, businesses must move at the same pace as the market they operate in, courting the attention of consumers, establishing a relationship with them and

9. Joseph Schumpeter, *Capitalism, Socialism and Democracy*, George Allen & Unwin Ltd, 1976, p82.
10. Romesh Vaitilingam, 'Overview: The Economics of the Knowledge Driven Economy', in papers from *The Economics of the Knowledge Driven Economy*, conference organised by the DTI and the Centre for Economic Policy Research, 27.1.99, www.dti.org/, p5.

tailoring their products accordingly (customer capital). Such organisations need to become 'just-in-time' enterprises in which the paradigm of 'make and sell' is transformed into 'sense and respond.'[11] The old style of mass marketing, and functional modes of thinking which prohibit rapid adaptation, have to be updated and changed by experiment. In this 'attention economy', customer information is gathered and integrated into a business's mode of production, enabling it to continuously attune its products and marketing to highly specific constituencies. The internet now offers the possibility of popularising build-to-order - mass customising products for individual consumers. The knowledge-driven economy is contingent, unstable and globalised; the homogenised cultures of mass production and consumption are fragmenting. Corporations which have built strong, singular global brands are now losing market share, as consumers reject them in favour of more local, culturally specific brands: between 2000 and 2001 the market value of Coca Cola fell 5 per cent; McDonalds by 9 per cent; and Nike by 5 per cent.[12]

The cultural revolution in production, and the need to acquire and utilise human, intellectual and customer capital, has led a majority of leading firms to practise knowledge management. Hubert Saint-Onge, a leading theorist, describes intellectual capital as the management of intangible assets: 'We know that these assets now represent the largest share of the value of most firms and that we need to manage these assets actively in order to optimise the performance of organisations in their respective market place.'[13] But as Lars Hakenson writes in the *European Business Forum*, 'Knowledge obtains economic significance only through application in the performance of an economically meaningful activity, i.e. the exercise of a skill.'[14] The main source of productivity is the ability to 'codify' knowledge in order to effectively apply, manage, measure and commodify it: 'by its very nature tacit knowledge is often the basis of a competitive

11. See 'Conversation with Hubert Saint-Onge, Senior Vice President for Strategic Capabilities, Clarica Life Insurance Company', Jay Chatzkel, *Journal of Intellectual Capital*, www.progressivepractices.com. On production as 'build-to-order', see Christiane Schulzki-Haddouti, 'Up close and personalised' in *connectis*, issue 11, May 2001, supplement to the *Financial Times*; DTI's Foresight paper on 'The Attention Economy and the C2C Economy: two new online markets', www.foresight.gov.uk.
12. Richard Tomkins, 'No Logo' in the *Financial Times*, 7.8.01.
13. Quoted by Jay Chatzkel, full reference n.11.
14. Lars Hakanson, 'The Rediscovery of Articulation', *European Business Forum*, issue 5, Spring 2001, www.ebfonline.com.

advantage'.[15] Michael Polanyi, whose book *Personal Knowledge, Toward a Critical Epistemology* (1958) has been a seminal influence in knowledge management, differentiated between explicit or codified knowledge, focused upon an object or phenomenon, and a more fundamental, unreflected form of tacit knowledge ('knowledge about knowledge'), which underlies it. Creating value and increasing productivity involves 'articulating' tacit knowledge into usable, codified information.[16]

Neither a simple audit of a company's intellectual capital, nor the installation of new information and communication technologies will guarantee an increase in profits - as many companies have discovered to their cost, when substantial investment in ICTs has yielded no obvious benefit in levels of productivity. As Erik Brynjolfsson has noted, 'the same dollar spent on the same system may give a competitive advantage to one company but only expensive paper weights to another.'[17] The 'articulation' and exploitation of knowledge for the creation of wealth demands investment in human capital, and that requires a culture of learning, innovation and creativity. What counts is the capacity of a company to manage discontinuous change by redefining its organisation in order to exploit its employees' intellectual and technical aptitudes. The US corporate education research group Corporate University Xchange estimates that over the past fifteen years the number of corporate universities has swelled from about 400 to some 2000:[18] 'A corporate university is formed when a corporation seeks to relate its training and development strategies to its business strategy by co-ordination and integration and by the development of intellectual capital within the organisation in pursuit of its corporate aims and objectives'.[19] Since Motorola's pioneering effort, corporate universities are no longer confined to training and educating employees. Increasingly, senior management uses them to instil corporate values and loyalty in employees, and also to enhance customer

15. David Coates and Ken Warwick, Chief and Senior Economic Advisers DTI, 'The Knowledge Driven Economy: Analysis and Background', in *The Economics of the Knowledge Driven Economy*, p12 (full reference n.10).
16. For example, see Knowledge Consultant Karl-Erik Sveiby, www.sveiby.com.au.
17. Erik Brynjolfsson, *Information Week*, 9.9.96, quoted in 'Knowledge Management for the New World of Business', Yogesh Malhotra, 1998, www.brint.com.
18. Linda Anderson, 'Tailor-made for life-long learning', *Business Education Supplement*, *Financial Times*, June 4, 2001.
19. *Corporate Universities - Learning Partnerships for the Future*, Henley Management College 2000, quoted in *The Future of Corporate Learning*, DTI, DfEE, www.dti.gov.uk.

capital by providing consumers with e-learning access to the corporation.

Corporate universities are a growing response to the need for a learning organisation responsive to market change. They provide an education sourced from knowledge generated internally and structured in response to immediate business needs. John Neill, CEO of the Unipart Group, praises its online learning system because it enables employees 'to learn at the speed of light'.[20] Short-term, cost-effective gain is the priority. However, there are long-term costs involved in depending upon such a system, tied to existing products and capital investment. The procedure-driven, utilitarian logic of business breaks down tacit knowledge into easier-to-use, codified information. The emphasis on employees acquiring the coded information, for example the scripts used in call centres, is simply a continuation of Taylor's principles of Scientific Management. Learning is by rote, reduced to a performance, subject to measurement and linked to productivity. The consequence for the whole organisation is an undermining of creativity and the depletion of tacit knowledge. Tina Poulon, senior manager for group training at PricewaterhouseCoopers, has warned against this kind of corporate education: 'just putting materials on the web doesn't mean people are going to learn.'[21] Corporate cultures organised around optimising output undermine the kind of plural, open and sharing associations necessary for knowledge creation. Critical reflection on the part of employees is narrowly confined to the level of understanding relations and processes internal to the organisation's systems.

This new world of knowledge-based industries emphasises a constantly evolving adaptation, and recourse to intuitive forms of thinking. Most firms are hierarchical and culturally conservative, however, and their central dilemma is how to reconstruct their organisations internally to meet this challenge. The economist Alfred Marshall's description of economic districts - creating clusters of industries in response to 'ideas in the air' - has been revived to explain the structural development of the knowledge-driven economy. Clusters encourage 'social capital' in the form of mutual support and co-ordination and the sharing of 'know how'. The idea of the network society has extended itself into the internal organisation of corporations, where management theorists talk about flattening hierarchies, sharing knowledge, and building

---

20. Quoted in Government White Paper on Enterprise, Skills and Innovation, Chapter 2, 2001, www.dti.gov.uk.
21. Tina Poulon quoted in 'Skills crisis 2001 - more questions than answers', www.silicon.com/skills_survey_2001

communities of practice. However, the limitations of corporate and vocational training mean that knowledge capitalism must draw upon non-commodity forms of education, culture and social relations, which value creativity and imagination. The European Commission's First Action Plan on Innovation in Europe recognised that a new compact between the market and society is required: 'Cultural attitudes, the economic environment, the social context and the educational and legal structures are key factors in the spirit of innovation and enterprise.' [22]

The changes in the means of production and the need to lever knowledge through learning and application are encouraging more fierce attempts to run society as an adjunct of the market. The Marxist critic Georg Lukacs declared, in 1919, 'thanks to its commodity and communications arrangements capitalist society has given the whole of economic life an identity notable for its autonomy, its cohesion and its exclusive reliance on immanent laws.' [23] These laws, Lukacs adds, are 'entirely unconnected with man's humanity', reducing individuals to numbers and numerical relations. The development of capitalism in the nineteenth century subordinated society to the governing principle of exchange value, creating markets out of natural and human resources. Social relations were embedded in the economic system. The earlier waves of the industrial revolution witnessed the enclosures of the commons, as labour and land were commodified. In order for them to be bought and sold they became, along with money, fictitious commodities. [24] In today's most advanced information economies, knowledge and learning are being turned into fictitious commodities. The knowledge corporations are engaged in a contemporary version of the enclosures, as the market and the exercise of intellectual property rights take over from the traditional elites, to reconfigure and restrict access to the intellectual commons.

New Labour and corporate power

New Labour's response to the knowledge driven economy was contained in its 1998 Competitiveness White Paper, *Our Competitive Future - Building the*

---

22. Quoted in *Job Creation and Competitiveness through Innovation*, 1998, p13, the European Round Table of Industrialists, www.ert.be.
23. Georg Lukacs, 'The Changing Function of Historical Materialism', in *History and Class Consciousness: Studies in Marxist Dialectics*, trans. Rodney Livingstone, Merlin Press 1971, p231.
24. Karl Polanyi, *The Great Transformation*, Beacon Press 1957, pp72-73.

Knowledge Driven Economy. Peter Mandelson, Minister of Trade and Industry, delivered the New Labour position: 'Knowledge and its profitable exploitation by business is the key to competitiveness'. But, he confessed to the TUC, despite a world-class science base, and talent and creativity galore, the country lacked entrepreneurs able to turn these natural strengths into products and services.[25] To galvanise a new competitive spirit required the promotion of an entrepreneurial culture. Charles Leadbeater, one of the authors of the White Paper, advised New Labour that 'education is the first priority, a policy for mass entrepreneurship is the second.'[26] His priorities were adopted in the Department of Trade and Industry's 2001 White Paper on Enterprise, Skills and Innovation, which ensured that 'creativity, enterprise and the ability to innovate are at the heart of the education and skills we provide to our young people and adults'. New Labour has committed itself to a competitive, post-welfare state, and the marketisation of the public sector, priorities which mirror the strategic goals of European big business.

The 2000 Lisbon European Council on employment, economic reform and social cohesion committed Europe to a new strategic goal: 'to become the most competitive and dynamic knowledge based economy in the world'.[27] The outcome of the summit was a triumph for a discreet lobby group, the European Round Table of Industrialists. Former ERT Secretary General Keith Richardson described the Lisbon summit as the peak of its influence on European policy making.[28] Founded in 1983, the ERT is an organisation of 48 chairpersons and CEOs of Europe's largest transnational corporations.[29] In 1998, its Competitiveness Working Group, under the chairmanship of Baron Daniel Janssen, published *Job Creation and Competitiveness through Innovation*, providing a definitive statement by big business on building a new competitive society in response to globalisation.[30]

25. Speech to the TUC, 17.9.98, www.dti.gov.uk
26. Charles Leadbeater, *Living on Thin Air*, Penguin 2000, p243.
27. Lisbon European Council Presidency Conclusions, 23-24 March 2000, www.europa.eu.int/comm/index_en.htm.
28. Keith Richardson, *Big Business and the European Agenda*, Sussex European Institute, SEI Working Paper No. 35, www.sussex.ac.uk
29. For more information see www.ert.be. Together with its more formal fellow organisation, the Union of Industrial and Employers Confederations of Europe (UNICE), the ERT has arguably been the ideological driver for EU economic development. See also *Corporate Europe Observer* for detailed analyses and data on corporate involvement in EU politics, www.xs4all.nl/~ceo/.
30. www.ert.be.

The report offers a culture of innovation as the panacea for Europe's perceived failure to match the productivity levels of the US economy. Stale and hidebound ways of thinking will be swept away, competitiveness boosted, and new, as yet indefinable, markets created. European culture is faulted for favouring 'greater security, stability and equality over risk-taking, creativity and innovation'. The report concludes that there is a 'crying need for greater flexibility in labour laws at a national level in Europe'. Fixed-wage structures stifle change: 'We need to move away from a fixed-wage-earning society to a performance linked compensation system'. The Presidency Conclusions for the Lisbon Council adopt a similar logic, concluding that 'achieving the new strategic goal will rely primarily on the private sector, as well as on public-private partnerships.'[31]

Trade in education

In January 2001, Lord Sainsbury told the North West Knowledge Economy Conference that the universities were at the heart of the UK's productive capacity: 'they are the hub of the business networks and industrial clusters'.[32] Quoting Tony Blair's Oxford *Romanes* speech on education, he announced that 'entrepreneurial universities will be as important as entrepreneurial businesses, the one fostering the other'. Since the 1992 deregulation of universities, government prescription has brought them into closer conformity with the needs of business. Officially 'private sector bodies', universities increasingly function like commercial organisations, pursuing market share in competition with each other, favouring departments and research which can realise financial returns, and closing down low recruiting subject areas. Marketisation and performance management practices centralise regulation, measurement and quality control. Cuts in state funding encourage the use of the Private Finance Initiative and a transfer of publicly owned infrastructure to privately owned corporations. In the Higher Education Funding Council of England's booklet *Private Investment in Higher Education*, Chairman Sir Michael Checkland writes: 'Investment in higher education gives the private sector the opportunity to join in this success'.[33]

The knowledge economy acting on local service sectors is producing global

---

31. Presidency Conclusions, full reference n.27.
32. Ministers' Speeches, www.dti.gov.uk.
33. www.hefce.ac.uk.

commodities. In 1999, Mike Moore, Director General of the WTO, told the Third Debis Conference in Berlin that 'an ever increasing range of essentially local services' are being transformed into internationally tradable products: 'financial and business services, and education and health services are cases in point.'[34] The global market in education is made possible by the new information and communication technologies and the liberalisation of trade. A crucial factor has been the deregulation of domestic economies, which has had a huge impact on the development of the international financial markets which power globalisation. The OECD's *Recent Privatisation Trends* notes that privatised companies are often the most valuable firms in their markets: 'Recent research has demonstrated a huge impact of privatisation on the development of stock markets.'[35] In the US, for-profits universities are attracting Wall Street investment, and big conglomerates of universities are acting as brokers for their distance learning courses. A number of British universities are copying their American counterparts and setting themselves up in global consortia. Universitas 21 is an incorporated company of eighteen universities in ten countries, amongst them Nottingham, Glasgow, Edinburgh and Birmingham. It describes its 'core business' as the 'provision of a pre-eminent brand for educational services'. Its aim is to 'leverage the reputation, resources and experience of its members on behalf of corporate partners.'[36] In Britain, high-tech vendors like Oracle, Cisco, IBM and Compaq are establishing roots in UK academic institutions. Sodexho is one of the growing number of global corporations who are developing 'bundled services' to exploit the increasing access to public sector services markets through outsourcing and PFIs. Global consultancy firms like KPMG are providing private sector advice to universities redesigning their systems of corporate governance and procurement.

The integration of higher education into the global market demonstrates the importance of the liberalisation of trade in services and intellectual property in the development of the knowledge economy. In the late 1990s the World Trade Organisation focused its attention on two multilateral agreements: Trade-Related Aspects of Intellectual Property Rights (TRIPS) and the General Agreement in Trade and Services (GATS). Both are part of the 'built in' agenda of the WTO, which describes GATS as 'the world's first multilateral agreement on investment,

---

34. www.wto.org/speeches.
35. *Recent Privatisation Trends 1999*, www.oecd.org.
36. www.universitas.edu.au.

since it covers not just cross-border trade but every possible means of supplying a service, including the right to set up a commercial presence in the export market.'[37] US corporations have played a decisive role in shaping its agenda. According to the WTO, in 1996 US exports of education services were estimated at US $7 billion. Fifty-eight per cent of its export market is Asia - Japan, China, Korea, Taiwan, India, Malaysia and Indonesia. Not only does the global trade in education have a huge growth potential, it is also highly strategic for the US in geopolitical terms. The key influence on the US Trade Representative's proposals on trade in education is the National Committee on International Trade in Education.[38] NCITE operates through the US Coalition of Service Industries (CSI), formed in 1982 with the aim of achieving greater liberalisation and access to foreign markets for US business. Its members include Anderson, Goldman Sachs, KPMG, Morgan Stanley Dean Witter and PricewaterhouseCoopers. The CSI offers prospective members the opportunity to develop relationships with key officials of international organisations such as the WTO and European Commission.[39] The prizes are colossal. Education alone as a global wide industry tops $1 trillion dollars in public spending. Global inequalities in trade in knowledge are demonstrated by the US balance of trade in intellectual property, which was worth over $20 billion in 1995. In the same year Mexico and Brazil ran a deficit of almost $1billion. TRIPS will consolidate pre-existing conventions on intellectual property rights, universalising the legislation of the richest nations, to the detriment of the less industrialised world.[40]

---

37. Secretariat, www.wto.org. For research papers on GATS see *The Threat to Higher Education*, Jess Worth, Campaigns Officer for student pressure group www.peopleandplanet.org; *The WTO and the Millennium Round What is at stake for Public Education?* joint publication by Education International (www.ei-ie.org) and Public Services International (www.world-psi.org), available to download from EI. Clare Joy, GATS campaign officer at the World Development Movement has written an excellent paper, available online from www.wdm.org.uk. For a detailed introduction to GATS, see Allyson M. Pollock and David Price, 'Rewriting the regulations: how the World Trade Organisation could accelerate privatisation in health-care systems', in *The Lancet*, Vol. 356, 912.00.
38. www.tradeineducation.org/, see also Global Alliance for Transnational Education, www.odugato.org/.
39. www.uscsi.org, for example of links with World Bank, US politics, OECD and WTO see list of speakers and advisers for World Services Congress 1, November 1999. Participants on the Education and Training Panel were members of the NCITE steering committee.
40. www.wto.org; and Carlos M. Correa, Intellectual Property Rights, the WTO and Developing Countries (Zed Books, 2000)

In a restricted document, the WTO describes the UK process in Higher Education as 'a movement away from public financing and toward greater market responsiveness, coupled with increasing openness to alternative financing mechanisms, [which has] led universities in new directions, balancing academic quality with business management.'[41] Sergio Marchi, Chair of the WTO Council for Trade in Services, which oversees GATS, argues that such reforms are 'creating the conditions and desirability for further GATS liberalisation'.[42] In the meantime, New Labour's first term saw public expenditure in education at its lowest level in forty years.[43] In their uncritical embracing of knowledge capitalism, governments have provided it with access to publicly created social, cultural and human capital, without any obligation that it should be paid for through an increased taxation on profits. The Local Futures Group, casting a sceptical eye over the regional disparities of the UK knowledge economy, has revealed the consequences. Six million people - roughly one in six of the population - are without any formal educational qualifications. 'All the evidence indicates that the UK economy lacks the capacity to generate good jobs - by European standards - evenly across the regions.'[44]

A new political economy of knowledge

'What's interesting about the knowledge economy', remarks the US economist Paul Romer, 'is that we haven't figured out what the optimal institutions are. That's still a wide open question. What is the best way to structure our economic world?' [45] At the heart of how knowledge behaves as an economic resource lies the contradiction between the intellectual commons and intellectual property rights. As Romer argues, 'you can't have both strong property rights and competition'. Markets have operated on the basis of a relatively free availability of information.

---

41. The unnamed document was prepared for the Council for Trade in Services and provides background information for discussion on the education and training services sector. Check WTO site for posting.
42. Sergio Marchi, 'Climate of the WTO Services 2000 Negotiations', Speaking Notes for an Address to the Services 2000 Business-Government Dialogue, 15.11.00, Conference hosted by US Department of Commerce; text from speeches at www.wto.org.
43. See research by Howard Glennerster of the LSE, *Guardian*, 4.9.01.
44. 'The Geography of Economic Citizenship in Britain: A Reply to the Opportunity for All White Paper', Local Futures Group, 3 Queen Square, London WC1N 3AU, www.localfutures.com.
45. Joel Kurtzman, 'An Interview with Paul Romer', First Quarter 1997, www.strategy-business.com/thoughtleaders/97110/page1.html.

In the knowledge economy, information itself is embedded in the market structure and its availability is thus costed and restricted. The functioning of knowledge as a fictitious commodity differs from that of a manufactured good in that the latter relies for its value on its 'excludability' - if one person possesses it another cannot. This is not the case with knowledge. Digital data, for example, is cheap and easy to copy for free. Nor is knowledge as a product transparent: in education, and in the complicated world of information systems, it is not always possible to know what one wants, and to see what is on offer. The market, by apportioning value to information that is regulated, scarce or in exclusive ownership, creates monopolies that may prove very difficult to break down. Intellectual property is the motor of capital accumulation, but strong intellectual property rights undermine competition. Knowledge in commodity form will usurp the traditional means by which the market has managed property rights and exchange. Furthermore, information, ideas and concepts which are not embedded or encoded in institutions are 'non-rivalrous' goods - their use value does not diminish when they are shared. On the contrary, sharing information in a networked economy can increase their use value. The former Chief Economist at the World Bank, Joseph Stiglitz, is sceptical of a free market in knowledge: the 'fact that knowledge is, in central ways, a public good and that there are important externalities means that exclusive or excessive reliance on the market may not result in economic efficiency.'[46]

The knowledge driven economy is about more than leveraging the productive capacity of information. As with the enclosures of the nineteenth century and the development of manufacturing industry, we are witnessing a significant change in the nature of the market and a restructuring of its relationship to society. History has taught us that the enclosures generated widespread popular resistance, which resulted in society attempting to protect itself against the perils of the self-regulating market system. As knowledge capitalism commodifies parts of the intellectual commons, it will usurp the authority of traditional educated elites and effect a wider distribution and increased productivity of certain forms of knowledge. But, driven by the new ICTs, it will pursue the principle of optimal performance, absorbing cultural meanings, symbols and knowledge from the common stock of cultures, even from the substance of life itself. What's at stake is

---

46. Joseph Stiglitz, 'Knowledge in the Modern Economy', in The Economics of the Knowledge Driven Economy, pp54-55, full reference n.10.

not simply the privatisation of public services and the commercialisation of learning but the value society places on human conviviality. In the past the intellectual commons was monopolised as a source of class cultural and political authority. Now, the threat comes from knowledge corporations driven by commercial gain. In this second term of the Blair government, the knowledge economy as it is presently unfolding is antithetical to a learning society. We are living through a period of transition which offers the left an opportunity to redefine the relationship of the market to society. Reasserting a belief in the democratic right of access to, and control over, the common wealth of knowledge might just mark the beginning of the end of the long interregnum of the left.

Thanks to Michael Rustin for his advice and comments.

At the edge of asylum

Les Back

Les Back reflects on chaos and progress.

The alarms are going off, again. The patient lies still, lifeless except for the shallow movement caused by the rhythm of each breath. One of cruel ironies of intensive care is that those in most distress are deprived of a voice. The failing body speaks through the frequency of electronic pulses: alarms that signal readings on the life support machines. The nurses interpret these mute traces. Like profane seraphs they carry a burden that is beyond the call of duty. 'That is what the nurses, who are of all colours, suffer from: supererogatory love', writes Martin Amis. 'It overflows in them and so they have to come here and do all this.'[1]

Walter Benjamin commented famously that Paul Klee's painting 'Angelus Novus' could be viewed as a metaphor for history: 'progress' corresponded to something close to an anarchic piling up of human debris at the feet of the Angel. This powerful image looms as New Labour preens itself in power and rewards the 'Mandarins of Millbank' who lead it. But a storm is brewing. The details of its proportions are documented through the intimate witness provided by those who work at the bedside of the afflicted.

Nurses who experience the daily pressures of skill shortages, understaffing and patient disappointment are perhaps the best contemporary substitute for Klee's Angel. They oversee the human consequences that follow from the politician's 'weasel words', and from the lack of adequate resources in the National Health Service. But they also administer, document and take readings on the magnitude of the tempest. 'The angel would like to stay, awaken the dead, and make whole

---

1. Martin Amis, *Experience*, Vintage 2001, p341.

what has been smashed', wrote Benjamin.[2] But ultimately she is confounded and cannot repair what is broken. Fragment is heaped upon fragment and the relentless energy that is released drives movement forward without purpose.

Perhaps you can spend too much time in hospitals. More and more they seem to me places of internment and disposal. Benjamin's desperate refrain is perhaps a diagnosis of the present, rather than a metaphor for history. The nurses and doctors, whose endeavours are in good faith, simply can't 'make whole what has been smashed'. After a long day-shift in the eye of the storm a 'modern Angel' offered another haunting tale from ICU. It concerned an unknown man who died today from massive head injuries. No-one knew exactly what happened to him. It was certain that he was an Asylum Seeker. In his clothes were military papers that identified him as a former member of the Iraqi Army. Some assumed he must have been a deserter. Why else would he be trying to enter the United Kingdom through the channel tunnel on foot? No-one can be sure. The details of his story were erased as his life ebbed away. What is known is that he sustained his injuries in a fatal attempt to hitch a ride on a train. No-one knew his name, and few will ever hear his story.

New Labour has held firm against the 'aliens' whose desperation impels them to attempt 'walking under water'. Their authoritarian displays are aimed to boost focus group ratings. For they know that immigration is the only issue where the moribund Tories can hold consistently the upper hand. Such tough asylum postures are justified in the name of pragmatism. But they simply don't believe their own rhetoric. And somehow this is worse. It is worse because for them intolerance is not a matter of grim commonsense held sincerely. Rather, they solicit hate in bad faith. These displays of firmness on the issue of Asylum are just a means to covert public opinion.

Fleeing from the Nazis and refused entry to Spain at the village of Porbou, Walter Benjamin killed himself with a overdose of Morphine. He had made the long trek over the Pyrenees carrying his precious manuscript and life work - what was to become the Arcades Project - in a suitcase. The Spanish border police sent him back but there could be no return. Exhausted, he took the decision to, as Marshall Berman has written, make a 'pre-emptive strike on himself'.[3] Tragically,

2. Walter Benjamin, 'Theses on the Philosophy of History', in *Illuminations*, Fontana 1973, p249.
3. Marshall Berman, *Adventures in Marxism*, Verso 1999, p240.

the very next day his fellow asylum seekers were allowed entry into Spain and took flight. In 1994 the townspeople of Portbou erected a monument to Benjamin's memory. Engraved in stone are his words:

> It is more arduous to honour the memory of the nameless than that of the renowned. Historical construction is devoted to the memory of the nameless.

Benjamin's words venerate the mute voices of those who are - like the unknown Iraqi - fatally caught at the edge of asylum. But, the grinning impostors of politics, who hide from culpability, sleep better because the nameless are kept out of sight. They have no name, therefore they do not exist. The cruel truth is that, on each ward round, those who nurse the afflicted, both named and anonymous, are left to preside over a storm that hurtles them forward. Public sector burn-out, skills shortages in the NHS, the British National Party polling 12,000 votes in Oldham, civil unrest in Bradford, Tony Blair awarding himself a £50,000 pay increase - all are readings from the barometer of public life. Echoing Benjamin's prophecy we might ask: is this tumult 'what we call progress'?

Flexploitation strategies

UK lessons from and for Europe

Anne Costello and Les Levidow

The authors analyse and document struggles against the neoliberal 'flexibility' agenda.

There is nothing necessarily dignified about manual labour at all, and most of it is absolutely degrading. It is mentally and morally injurious to man to do anything in which he does not find pleasure...

Oscar Wilde, *The Soul of Man under Socialism*

Whose flexibility?

Labour 'flexibility' is always a relation of class struggle. Historically, such flexibility has sometimes provided a bargaining weapon against capitalist work-discipline. Since the 1980s, however, labour has been newly flexibilised to intensify its exploitation. Often called casual labour or *precarité*, this flexploitation imposes insecurity, indignity and greater discipline.

Flexploitation also intensifies inequalities along race and gender lines. Ethnic minority workers suffer great unemployment and greater cyclical fluctuations in employment; they are marginalised into the more insecure, subordinate jobs. So are women, especially those who need part-time work, which gives them inferior status, lower pay and less security.

A neoliberal form of flexibility has been officially justified as necessary to protect employment from competitive threats. When governments deregulate labour markets - for example by weakening legislation that once protected job security - employers can more readily eliminate jobs or replace workers with others on less secure contracts. They can more readily throw workers into competition with each other, thus extracting more labour at times and places more convenient for the production process, perhaps paying less wages overall than before. In this way, the creation of precarious forms of 'employment' provides a strategy for intensifying work discipline and extracting more work from everyone.

Multinational companies (MNCs) have a double-edged role in flexploitation strategies. On the one hand, their size can facilitate worker resistance and so set limits on exploitation. On the other hand, their geo-political scope can facilitate the transfer of work across the globe and/or to subcontractors, thus throwing their workforce and suppliers into greater competition. Thus small-sized companies too become instruments of these pressures, e.g. as competitors or subcontractors.

Such pressures and threats are used strategically in order to discipline wage labour. Of course, governments cite national dependence upon foreign investment as their reason for offering companies incentives such as tax breaks, subsidies and the deregulation of labour-market or environmental protection: such policies have been well documented for Third World countries. But they operate within Western countries too, though of course this is not mainly in order to accommodate external pressures, as is officially claimed.

Competition for investment or trade is not a plausible motive for labour-market deregulation, especially at the European level. Although OECD reports accepted the link between job loss and labour-market rigidities in the early 1990s, later reports cast doubt on that link. To quote one expert: 'Many labour-market institutions that conventionally come under the heading of rigidities have no observable impact on unemployment'.[1] Furthermore, only approximately 10 per cent of the European economy involves external trade. Contrary to official policy statements, trade liberalisation is promoted in order to intensify competitive pressures, discipline labour, extract more work and thus increase profitability.

---

1. H. Nickell, 'Labour market rigidities: at the root of unemployment in Europe', *Jnl of Economic Perspectives* 11(3), 1997, p73.

The real motives for labour flexibilisation can be seen by analysing the European Union and the United Kingdom in particular. This essay will make the following arguments:

◆ EU integration has been bound up with flexploitation agendas
◆ the UK has provided a Europe-wide impetus and model for them
◆ some trade unions have internalised and enforced flexploitation agendas
◆ resistance (in some ways) has gone beyond demands for waged labour
◆ a Europe-wide resistance can learn from the UK experience, and vice versa.

European neoliberal policies within 'partnership'

As a result of labour and political struggles, most European countries had adopted laws protecting workers' rights by the early 1980s. Although the protections varied, they generally included the following: the right to claim unfair dismissal shortly after starting a new job; limits on renewals of fixed-term contracts; regulations on the use of employment agencies; mandatory redundancy payments; pro-rata entitlements for part-time workers.

Such laws hardly exist in the USA, where workers can be sacked at will unless they have a contract that contains a 'just cause' standard. The USA does have laws prohibiting some kinds of discrimination - and thus discriminatory redundancy - on the basis of race, gender, age, or trade union involvement. But these laws are notoriously unenforced, weak, and getting weaker. Job security and fair treatment therefore depend upon the power of trade unions.

As another instance of transatlantic difference in legislation, recent EC Directives have drawn upon various national laws to set minimum European standards. And the co-determination procedure officially recognises the European Trade Union Confederation (ETUC) as social partners, with the employers' organisation (UNICE), in a dialogue which precedes the drafting of such Directives. Trade unions are also regarded as important for ensuring the implementation of Directives in each workplace, as for example with the EC Working Time Directive, which sets a 48-hour weekly limit. (The UK government obtained an exemption from this Directive so that individual UK workers may voluntarily 'choose' an opt-out from that limit.)

However, there has been a general change of direction in the aims of employment protection Directives since the 1980s. Originally such Directives were intended to avoid 'social dumping' across countries, thus achieving a 'social Europe'. But more recently they have been used as a tool to help bring about a framework for neoliberal policies, for example labour flexibilisation.

Flexibility for 'competitiveness'

The overall neoliberal agenda was heavily influenced by industry lobbyists from the European Round Table of Industrialists (ERT), founded in 1983. In particular the ERT promoted European Monetary Union (EMU) as a means to impose neoliberal policies. In pursuit of this aim, the 1991 Maastricht Treaty incorporated convergence criteria for budget deficits and inflation - limits which could be achieved only by cutting social welfare budgets, and by labour flexibilisation to restrict wages and reduce unit labour costs.[2]

To accommodate social democratic critics of EMU, the Social Chapter offered some protection. For example it mandated rights regarding maternity pay, parental leave, part-time work and redundancy consultation. Even if fully implemented, however, the Social Chapter would not be of use in protecting overall job security.

Through the 1990s, moreover, EU labour-market policies were virtually written by industry lobbyists. The ERT had blamed labour-market rigidities for limiting European economic competitiveness and thus jeopardising employment. It promoted deregulation as the essential means to promote growth and thus expand employment.

As President of the European Commission, Jacques Delors basically accepted a neoliberal diagnosis in his 1993 White Paper, *Growth, Competitiveness, Employment*. The document counselled adaptation to inexorable competitive pressures: 'The pressure of the market-place is spreading and growing, obliging businesses to exploit every opportunity available to increase productivity and efficiency'. At the same time, Delors acknowledged that the necessary changes could cause problems of 'exclusion', due to inadequate skills or qualifications (especially because of his emphasis on the key role of information technology).[3]

2. See R.F Duran, *Contra l'Europa del Capital o Globalizacion Economica*, Talaca, Madrid 1997; excerpted as 'The Europe of Capital', in K. Abramsky (ed), *Restructuring and Resistance: Diverse Voices of Struggle in Western Europe*, pp28-91, 2001. (*Restructuring and Resistance* can be ordered from resresrev@yahoo.com.)
3. 'Growth, Competitiveness, Employment: The Challenges and Ways Forward into the 21st Century', *Bulletin of the European Communities*, supplement 6/93. Commission of the European Communities, Brussels 1993, pp92-3.

The need for compensatory measures to counter this 'exclusion' then opened the way for social democracy to collude with programmes which define social inclusion solely in terms of remunerative work, of any kind.

In 1995 the European Commission set up a Competitiveness Advisory Group (CAG), which included leading figures from the ERT. In 1996 its third report, *Enhancing European Competitiveness*, called for 'modernising' the labour market through greater flexibility in working hours, wage moderation and greater labour mobility.[4]

Accordingly, EU member states sought to deregulate labour markets, partly in order to achieve the convergence criteria for EMU: Portugal's Socialist government adopted policies for annualised hours, temporary contracts and multi-skilling; the French government introduced measures to weaken the job security of public sector workers.

Moreover, workforce-related measures have undermined labour protection in several EU countries (especially in the UK, discussed below). France raised the proportion of welfare recipients who are required to seek work; such 'job-seekers' must attend counselling interviews and have less scope for rejecting unsuitable jobs. Germany has been creating new jobs at subnormal wages for the unemployed, who must accept them or else lose benefit. By the late 1990s, most new employment in Spain was on fixed-term contracts, partly encouraged by subsidies for hiring the unemployed. In Italy the unemployed have been pressed to work as 'socially useful workers' on temporary contracts, often being used to privatise public services; in response, protests have demanded permanent public sector contracts at normal pay rates.

New social workhouse

Such measures - forcing unemployed people into badly paid, unpleasant and precarious work, all in the name of social inclusion - can be understood as creating 'a new social workhouse'. And they have sometimes succeeded in incorporating into labour intensification schemes those who are usually critical of the neoliberal agenda.

---

4. Cited in B. Balanyá et al, *Europe Inc.: Regional & Global Restructuring and the Rise of Corporate Power*, Pluto Press, London 2000 (co-authored by Ann Doherty, Olivier Hoedeman, Adam Ma'anit and Erik Wesselius); see Corporate European Observatory, http://www.xs4all.nl/~ceo.

In response, Europe-wide social movements have sought inclusion in civil society on their own terms. They have remained antagonistic towards the EU's institutional forms and its neoliberal policies at national level. At EU level the flexibilisation agenda became particularly contentious after workers' revolts in Germany and France during 1996-97. Consequently, in the run-up to the June 1997 Amsterdam Summit, trade unions and left parties proposed that the new EU treaty should include an Employment Chapter, formalising demands for full employment.

Industry lobbying weakened that proposal, however, so that ultimately the Employment Chapter served to undermine the aims of its original proponents. EU governments agreed 'to work towards developing a co-ordinated strategy for employment and particularly for promoting a skilled, trained and adaptable workforce and labour markets responsive to economic change' (Amsterdam Treaty, Article 109n); the Employment Chapter came to be underpinned by the same neoliberal agenda as all the other policy documents at the summit. The national governments undertook to promote 'flexible labour markets', so that the EU could 'remain globally competitive'. Accordingly, the EU recommended 'a restrictive restructuring of public expenditures ... to encourage investment in human capital, research and development, innovation and the infrastructure essential to competitiveness'.[5]

In these ways, European integration measures have accepted the putative link between job creation and competitiveness, in turn dependent upon labour-market deregulation and liberalisation. Such an agenda cites external threats as the imperative for internal change. For example, a further report portrays the world economy as generating economic insecurity, 'with an irresistible flow of newer, better or cheaper goods or services that is constantly making older products uneconomic or obsolete - along with the jobs attached to them'.[6] According to this diagnosis, public expenditure must be used to enhance labour-market flexibility and innovation.

A central slogan has been 'employability'. This means individual responsibility to be continuously trained and adapted to labour-market needs: unemployment is attributed to individual deficiencies. The 1997 Luxembourg Jobs Summit adopted

5. EU Presidency, *Presidency Conclusions from the Amsterdam Summit*, SN 150/97, Annex, 1997, pp10-13.
6. *Job Creation and Competitiveness through Innovation*, European Round Table of Industrialists, Brussels 1998; http://www.ert.be/, cited in Balanyá et al, see note 4.

'European Employment Guidelines', stating principles of employability, adaptability, entrepreneurship and equal opportunities. Also in 1997 the EU published *Modernising and Improving Social Protection in the EU*, which argued for making 'social protection more employment-friendly' and for changing 'unemployment insurance into employability insurance'. Another document posed the question, 'how to reconcile security for workers with the flexibility which firms need?' - while in actuality proposing mainly that workers should adapt.[7]

> 'through a focus on "employability", unemployment is attributed to individual deficiencies'

In response to trade union pressures, the European Commission did eventually draft a Directive on Fixed-Term Contracts (FTCs), which provides parity of conditions for temporary workers. This proposed that the conditions of workers on FTCs should be comparable to those of the bulk of workers employed by the same company on more secure contracts. However this Directive has a number of problems: for example, such a comparator would be missing in workplaces where FTCs are the norm, or where workers' contracts are issued by another company - for example by a subcontractor outside the scope of a relevant collective agreement. These examples show how the effects of rule changes are always dependent upon the strategies and relations of class forces.

In all these issues, the ETUC has largely accommodated the neoliberal agenda rather than challenged it. They have sought to play the role of a responsible 'social partner' with industry, as mandated by the Maastricht Treaty. Furthermore, the ETUC participates with industry in playing a role in economic policy with the European Central Bank; here they have co-operated in undertaking to promote monetary stability, market flexibility and employment, as mandated by the Amsterdam Council. In the face of a cross-national dispute such as the 1997 Renault-Vilvoorde redundancies, the ETUC simply argued about legalities and codes of conduct - rather than seeking to defend the right to employment.

In most individual EU countries, governments and employers have opted for a similar kind of strategy in relation to trade unions: they are largely incorporated into consultation structures. In the UK, by contrast, the neoliberal strategy has mainly sought to confront trade unions and attack their independence. Let us now examine

---

7. CEC Green Paper, 'New Forms of Work Organisation', 1997; http://www.eiro.eurofound.ie/1997/05/inbrief/eu9705131n.html

how the UK has served as a European vanguard for flexploitation.

UK as flexploitation model

In its role as vanguard of neoliberalism in Europe since the mid-1970s, the British state has defeated, disorganised and decomposed the industrial working class as it had developed in the Fordist-Keynesian era. It imposed that defeat by wielding several weapons - including decentralisation, privatisation, flexibilisation and criminalisation. During the 1980s large centres of unionised workers were broken up and/or weakened - by, for example, reducing state subsidies, closing plants, and privatising state-owned industries or parts of public services.

Public expenditure was given new priorities. Previously it had helped to provide relatively secure employment, even for those in unskilled jobs; but this type of expenditure was reduced in the name of controlling the national debt and reducing inflation. Eligibility rules for unemployment benefit were changed in order to push people into low-paid work. Casual labour became more common through an increase in the use of subcontractors or employment agencies (which are often owned by multinational companies).

UK neoliberalism had its origins in 1976-77. Back then the Labour government entered a phase of anti-worker policies: for example it enacted repressive laws and cut public expenditure. Subsequently the Government faced widespread working-class revolt, losing the 1979 election; the Conservative Party then resumed the task during its rule, which lasted till 1997.

Since then the New Labour government has continued the policy of low costs for employers and legal limits on trade union activity, as a means to achieve national competitiveness. In its 1997 election campaign, New Labour undertook to retain key elements of the Tory legislation. As the future Prime Minister proudly proclaimed, any changes would still 'leave British law the most restrictive on trade unions in the Western world' (*The Times*, 31.03.97). Indeed, accepting the UK's role as the sweatshop of Europe, the New Labour government has promoted its neoliberal policies as models for Europe and the EMU convergence criteria.

Deregulating the labour market

The process of labour-market deregulation has been driven by legislative changes. Prior to 1985, a worker could demand compensation for unfair dismissal after holding a job for six months, but the Tory government changed the minimum period to two years. During this time a worker could be dismissed for no reason, and without the right of appeal to an industrial tribunal. The new rule gave employers an extra incentive to dismiss new workers within the two-year limit, thus avoiding redundancy payments and industrial tribunal cases.

The consequent insecurity affects far more people than simply those working on fixed-term contracts. The 'two-year rule', providing freedom for employers to create insecure jobs, affects unemployed people in particular: more than half who find a job lose it again within a year. In 1999 the New Labour government changed the two-year limit for claiming unfair dismissal to one year, but this may only serve to give employers an incentive to dismiss people within one year.

Such pressures and insecurities have led workers to accept the carrying out of increasing levels of unpaid, or underpaid, labour, especially through overtime. Although some overtime is paid at premium rates, often it is not, especially for casual or part-time workers. Moreover, much overtime goes entirely unpaid. Employers can impose increased workloads by various means, for example by reducing the workforce but not the workload. According to one estimate, UK employers benefit annually from £23bn worth of unpaid labour, i.e. approx. 1k Euros per employee.

In addition to all this, EC Directives for employment protection have been implemented in a relatively weak way by the UK, as in the opt-out from the Working Time Directive. Another example of weak implementation in the UK is the EC Fixed-Term Work Directive, which regulates for equality of conditions (other than pay) between permanent and temporary workers. This Directive requires member states to restrict the length of time a worker can be employed on successive temporary contracts, as well as the number of successive contracts, and the circumstances in which they can be used. Accordingly, most EU countries have regulations limiting the use of successive temporary contracts to a total period of three years or less. However, the UK's draft regulations set a higher limit - four years. Even then the employer may still renew the contract as a fixed-term contract where there is 'objective justification' - thus allowing great scope to manage and even legitimise casualisation. (For example, 'uncertain funding' has been routinely cited to justify academic researchers being kept on a series of fixed-term contracts.) The UK draft regulations also define 'worker' as an 'employee', thus excluding self-employed people from the Regulations; and they use a restrictive definition of 'comparator' with permanent workers.

Penalising solidarity

Other Tory legislation imposed constraints and penalties upon traditional forms of class solidarity. Trade unions became liable to court actions by employers seeking to recover income lost due to strikes. Trade unions were required to hold a secret ballot before any strike action. Employers became legally entitled to sack all strikers en masse. (New Labour's 1999 legislation reversed this to some extent, by protecting strikers for the first eight weeks from the start of a legally permitted or 'protected' strike.)

Moreover, under Tory legislation it became illegal for workers to take 'secondary action' - i.e. against a company that is not their own employer. This prohibition remains in UK law. Consequently, employers split up their own companies and/or subcontracted their workforce, so that any solidarity action could be labelled 'secondary'. In various ways, some employers have phased out long-established unionised workers (or their posts), and replaced them with casualised ones. In some cases, employers recognise a trade union on condition that a proportion of the workforce remains on temporary contracts, so that the latter are excluded from collective bargaining procedures; this arrangement internalises the 'reserve army' within the company.

Together these weapons have disorganised and fragmented class resistance within trade unions. Shop stewards' organisations have been severely hampered by Tory laws which forbid strike action without advance notice and written ballots. Such organisations have often lost their independence as well as their power.

In its effects, the restrictive legislation has been more 'anti-solidarity' than 'anti-union'. Trade unions have often cited or used the restrictive legislation to police their own members. For example, after Tory laws restricted the numbers who could legally picket a workplace, some trade unions issued armbands to a few 'official' pickets; thus the police could more readily arrest the unofficial ones. Some trade unions have denied local requests for ballots, thus putting workers' actions outside the law.

Many trade unions have accommodated and even reinforced this class defeat. Under the 'New Realism', they have sometimes played the role of would-be 'partners' with management in order to recruit members on whatever terms possible. Although this partnership policy has been opposed by many left activists, it has been supported by most national leaders of trade unions, regardless of whether they are called left-wing or right-wing.

Fundamentally, trade unions face two conflicting options. They can either support resistance, especially after workers are collectively sacked, or else seek to recruit the casualised workers who replace them. Pursuing the latter option, some unions have actively undermined workers' resistance.

Making work for the unemployed

To discipline the workforce, the state has sought to flexibilise the unemployed too. They are kept busy in work-like activities, as a requirement for receiving unemployment benefits. From 1989 benefits have been withdrawn from anyone who refuses certain official 'training' schemes or a 'reasonable job'.

In particular, since 1996 unemployment benefit has been re-named the JobSeekers' Allowance (JSA), with lower benefit levels for people under 25 years old and means-testing after six months, rather than after twelve as before. Eligibility rules now require people to accept any job in any field at any legal wage, after three months of unemployment. They can also be denied benefit if they study on courses (chosen by them) for more than 16 hours per week, thus denying many unemployed youth an opportunity to improve their qualifications. A more extreme attack, Project Work, is a 'work-for-benefit' scheme, dating from 1996. Similar schemes form parts of the New Deal introduced by the New Labour government.

Although the Labour Party had criticised the Tory programme, the New Labour government extended it. Launched in 1998, the 'New Deal' drew on the ideology and practice of US workfare measures. Under the new rules, unemployed people under 25 can claim benefit for only six months before undergoing intensive counselling, designed to push them into low-paid work. Often employers prefer these workers to those who are older and better-paid, because the UK minimum wage law (also introduced in 1999) has lower rates for trainees and those under 21. If counselling fails, 'New Dealers' are offered a notional choice between subsidised waged work, usually in the private sector, low-level training, or a voluntary sector 'placement' paid at benefit level plus a small extra payment. A similar system is gradually being extended to the long-term unemployed over 25.

Through the New Deal, then, unemployed people face greater responsibilities and fewer rights (or eligibility). They are deterred from claiming benefits, and find themselves pushed towards McJobs, i.e. low-paid, temporary and part-time employment. Training and work schemes have served to impose discipline, to cheapen their labour, and to lower expectations.

Such changes further abandon the Keynesian model of social insurance and welfare, while adopting the US model of 'workfare'. These changes intensify the work of 'job-seeking', intensify competition among 'job-seekers', and so reduce their bargaining power. In abandoning the social democratic agenda of 'full employment', New Labour has substituted a neoliberal agenda of maximising employment and thus the labour supply for capital. Although Chancellor Gordon Brown has claimed that UK government policies offer 'the right to work', this really means a duty to work.

For example, until the late 1990s lone parents had an entitlement to a basic income without any work requirement, yet now they must attend compulsory 'work-focused interviews' to validate their benefit claim, once their youngest child is in school. This system is undergoing trial in selected areas, prior to national implementation by 2002. Both the Tories and New Labour have instituted policies to increasingly narrow the eligibility for disability payments, so that many people with disabilities must now seek paid employment. The 'work-focused interview' system now extends to them.

'Skills' too have been re-orientated towards flexibilisation. Vocational training for low-level skills proliferates new certificates, which are aimed at enhancing 'employability'; yet these can stigmatise those who have no other formal qualifications, while intensifying competition for jobs. 'Life-long learning', which likewise has been promoted by the ERT, becomes a perpetual responsibility to acquire new skills; consequently, 'the workers of tomorrow will be able to recycle themselves at their own expense during their free time', as one critic argues.[8]

Like its predecessor, the New Labour government has pushed the higher education sector to increase student numbers. Yet it has imposed tuition fees, while offering students only loans rather than grants. To limit their debts, students swell the many applicants for low-paid, part-time jobs, thus allowing employers to minimise wages and job security.

As agreed at the Amsterdam Summit, UK government expenditure has been directed at disciplining and flexibilising labour. The instruments include: expanding the New Deal beyond young people; encouraging 'inactive' people to accept any

---

8. N. Hirtt, 'The "Millennium Round" and the liberalisation of the education market', *Education and Social Justice* 2(2), 2000.

employment; and providing in-work benefits. Through the Working Families Tax Credit, for example, the government subsidises low wages - rather than forcing employers to increase them.

When New Labour re-introduced a minimum wage in 1999, it was designed to serve that neoliberal agenda. Its introduction raised the relative wages of the very lowest-paid workers, but this uplift is planned to cease by 2002, when further increases will barely keep pace with inflation. The once-off uplift was necessary to set a floor and thus to limit the overall state subsidy for low wages. By 'making work pay', moreover, the minimum wage ideologically justifies the stronger emphasis on the duty to work.

Work-discipline measures have gained support from trade union officials. Previously they had distanced themselves from the Tory workfare programmes; they had campaigned against the benefit cuts and rule changes associated with the Jobseekers' Allowance. After the 1997 election, however, they accepted New Labour claims that its version would provide social inclusion through 'the right to work'. Many national unions have co-sponsored the New Deal. Thus the government and trade unions have colluded in weakening limits on exploitation.

Unemployed people have organised resistance to the new social workhouse. Protest has deterred some charities from offering workfare-type 'placements' in Brighton, Hull and Edinburgh. In summer 1997 the Euromarch organised some occupations of job centres.[9]

Political responses by unemployed groups have varied. Most UK supporters of the European Marches demand the 'right to work' or 'full employment'. Others instead demand income, seeing no reason to demand their own exploitation.

Collective resistance by the precariously employed

Many employers have attacked and casualised their workforce with the help of neoliberal policies (for example the anti-solidarity legislation described above). They have found replacement workers to accept insecure and fixed-term contracts, thanks to the stricter conditions on seeking and accepting work imposed on the unemployed. Sooner or later, trade unions have sought to accommodate the casualisation regimes rather than resist them.

---

9. See A. Mathers, 'Resistance to workfare in the UK', in *Restructuring and Resistance*, pp407-11, see note 2.

Anti-solidarity legislation has sometimes provided a convenient pretext, or even a tool, for that accommodation. But a reverse logic can sometimes operate when trade unions have themselves internalised flexploitation strategies, as in the disputes at Hillingdon Hospital and the Liverpool docks.

Hillingdon dispute

The background to the Hillingdon dispute lies in the early 1980s, when the Tory government introduced compulsory competitive tendering (CCT). This regime forces public sector institutions to call for tenders for the running of specific services. The CCT requirement encourages such bodies to throw their workforce into competition with external bidders, to casualise their terms, and/or to replace them via subcontractors. The National Health Service has done so on a national scale, generally without much resistance.

A major exception was Hillingdon Hospital in the west London suburbs. Unionised cleaners and catering workers there, mainly Punjabi women, refused to sign a new contract from an employment agency, Pall Mall. The contract imposed a large pay cut; and it abolished pension rights, unsocial hours allowances, and employer sick pay. Pall Mall also humiliated the largely Asian workforce by demanding photocopies of their passports.

The workers who refused to sign were soon replaced by cheaper, non-union staff on short-term contracts from an employment agency. Although they were sometimes treated in racist ways, the strikers obtained support from the local Asian communities, from many local branches of their union, and strike pay from their national trade union. The strikers maintained a daily picket at the hospital - despite harassment, arrest and imprisonment. Their trade union, UNISON, initially attempted to discourage the strike, gave official backing only when it became unstoppable, and subsequently made little effort to support it or to recruit hospital staff.

In January 1997 UNISON announced that its support would cease and recommended that the strikers accept redundancy payments. According to an internal document from Pall Mall, the agency sought to 'normalise relations' with the union. According to the strikers' leader:

> When UNISON leaders signed a deal with Pall Mall, this was done without any ballot and behind the backs of the strikers. The reason given for this deal

was that the strike could not be won and that the strikers would also lose their forthcoming Industrial Tribunal.[10]

After UNISON ceased its regular payments to the strikers, their subsistence became dependent upon donations, and UNISON sought to dissuade its local and regional structures from helping to finance them. However the strikers continued their dispute, through continuing picket lines and attending political conferences around Europe. At the June 1998 UNISON conference, the national leadership was defeated by an overwhelming vote for a resolution that the union should restore official recognition, strike pay and full membership to the strikers. In response the national leadership put the Hillingdon strikers into a 'holding branch' which never meets, and restored 'hardship pay' in lieu of strike pay. The picketing continued on an unofficial basis, and UNISON promised to negotiate for jobs with the employer, but nothing materialised. (For more details, see Bilkhu's article, footnoted below.)

Eventually Pall Mall ran into financial problems, mainly because it had won NHS contracts on the basis of low tenders but then was not able to reduce wages and conditions as much as expected. The strikers won their Industrial Tribunal case against Pall Mall, which was then taken over by Granada. The new company appealed against the Tribunal decision but lost, and so had to pay compensation. In August 2000 Granada informed the union that jobs would become available for the strikers at Hillingdon. According to the strikers' leader: 'It shows the tremendous courage of a group of low paid, mainly Asian women workers who have not been intimidated by big employers like Granada, nor by opposition from UNISON leaders, representing the biggest union in the country' (see note 10 for reference). As this dispute shows, class resistance can disrupt financial calculations and so deter flexploitation strategies.

Solidarity beyond waged labour

As the Hillingdon dispute illustrates, some employers found that the consequences of flexploitation were more costly than anticipated, partly because of worker resistance. Since the mid-1990s, more and more workers have revolted against the degrading conditions, intensity, indignity and/or lower wages which characterise flexploitation.

---

10. M. Bilkhu, 'Hillingdon Hospital strike', in *Restructuring and Resistance*, pp252-54.

London Underground train drivers struck in summer 1996 over the employer's failure to implement a shorter working week - which had been promised a year earlier. Post Office workers struck for shorter hours and against employers' plans to intensify workloads and impose new 'work teams' to replace the existing ones. Food manufacturing and garment workers, especially from migrant groups (e.g. Turkish or Kurdish), held strikes in North East London during 1996; the strikers opposed unpaid and compulsory overtime, while demanding written contracts and union recognition.

Even when workers are sacked *en masse*, some have successfully continued their disputes by subsisting on strike pay, donations, unofficial work, etc. They often elude political control by their own unions. Although demanding the right to regain their former jobs, these ex-workers seek a dignity which has been lost from flexibilised jobs.

Such activity marks a cultural change from earlier periods of mass redundancies. In the past ex-workers related mainly to fellow trade union members or to Unemployed Workers Centres. By contrast, when workers resisted casualisation and were sacked *en masse* in the late 1990s, many became full-time political activists who related not only to similar disputes but to wider struggles beyond jobs and unemployment benefits.

Such strikers have been supported by a left core within the trade unions, as well as by various groups outside, e.g. anarchists, autonomists and environmentalists. Although the environmentalists may have jobs and perhaps hold trade union membership, their political identities are more likely to lie in developing resistance and alternatives to waged labour discipline. Many of them have no long-term attachment to particular jobs or trade unions. Together they resist efforts to re-integrate them into more subordinated, more disciplined and lower-paid jobs.

In the mid/late 1990s these new collectivities were recomposing class antagonism beyond waged labour. Such activity drew together people on the margins of the labour force. With an eye towards continental European struggles, some activists have used the term 'precarity' to link the related categories of unemployed, insecurely employed, part-time un/employed, workfare-conscripts and ex-workers demanding back their jobs. Such networks gave support to sacked workers in several disputes (for example the strikers at Hillingdon Hospital, Magnet Kitchens and the Liverpool docks), who also forged links with each other.

In 1996 the Magnet Kitchens factory in Darlington (North East England) sacked all 350 furniture workers after they went on strike. After the lock-out, the company spent more money on security guards than it would have cost to satisfy the pay rise which workers had demanded over the previous decade. For the company, to disorganise workers' solidarity was more important than to save money.

The management replaced the Magnet workers with low-paid strike-breakers, who soon became socially ostracised in the local area. Later they were given new contracts on even worse terms than before. Despite a national campaign and a consumer boycott, the sacked workers did not regain their jobs.

Through all these disputes, supporters carried out the following activities: occupying or picketing the employment agencies which had recruited strikebreakers; picketing the AGM of Magnet Kitchens and its local showrooms, especially to promote a consumer boycott; occupying the Labour Party headquarters to highlight the Hillingdon dispute, which was consequently featured on a TV news programme; and soliciting funds from local union branches and other organisations.

Solidarity activists came from two political cultures with different views of the disputes. For autonomist networks of the precariously employed, the disputes exemplified general struggles against wage-labour exploitation and capitalist work. From this view, the Campaign Linking Against Waged Labour (CLAWS) also built resistance to workfare programmes. For members of left parties, by contrast, the disputes exemplified the general struggle against casualisation. From this view, the London Support Group for the Liverpool Dockers appealed mainly to fellow trade union activists (see below). Although people from the two political cultures sometimes acted together, co-operation could be limited by their differences; these tensions were largely ignored rather than discussed.

Liverpool Dockers

During their 1995-98 dispute, sacked Liverpool dockers made great advances in generalising class solidarity, inspiring wider struggles against casualisation, both in Britain and abroad.[11] The dispute originated in 1989 Tory legislation which abolished the National Dock Labour Scheme which had previously protected British dockers from casual terms of employment. Once that

11. For more detail see: Mersey Docks Dispute (1995-97) webpage at http://www.geocities.com/CapitolHill/3843/dockhome.html; and M. Lavalette, and J. Kennedy, *Solidarity on Water: The Liverpool Lock-out of 1995-96*, Liver Press, Birkenhead 1996.

protection was removed, nation-wide casualisation ensued, which met organised resistance only from dockers in Liverpool. However, on the threat they all would be dismissed, the dockers eventually accepted new contracts, with longer, more 'flexible' shifts.

After the new contracts were signed, the MDHC continued to reduce and casualise the workforce. In the early 1990s many dockers' jobs were casualised through the use of an employment agency, Torside - which was in reality a creation of the MDHC. Under this arrangement, the MDHC could declare that they did not employ casual labour, because it was the new agency that handled the employment contracts. In the meantime the MDHC de-recognised the shop stewards elected by the long-standing workforce.

From 1989 onwards, the shop stewards repeatedly asked the national Transport & General Workers Union (TGWU) to arrange a ballot for strike action, as required by the Tory laws. However, the union always refused their request.[12] By denying a ballot, the leadership used the law to control the dockers and to put any strike action outside the law.

The dispute finally erupted in September 1995, when Torside workers struck against compulsory overtime for an inadequate rate of pay. They were instantly dismissed. MDHC employees refused to cross the picket line and were themselves dismissed. When the dockers sought to return to work, they found that their jobs had been taken by casual workers at much lower wages. Later, some of the sacked workers were offered new individual contracts on worse conditions than before, which they rejected. They were also offered large redundancy payments, which they also rejected.

Although their trade union (the TGWU) provided facilities and financial assistance, it refused to support actions against the MDHC, on the grounds that the original strikers had been employed by Torside. According to the TGWU, such support would thus be illegal under the Tory laws prohibiting 'secondary' action (see above). The sacked dockers came under ever greater pressure to settle the dispute - e.g. by accepting redundancy payments or by returning to work as casual labour. From late 1996 onwards, there was much discussion about how to establish a 'labour-hiring' system, in which the union would play the role of employment

<hr>

12. MPSSC (Merseyside Port Shop Stewards Committee), The Story of 500 Sacked Liverpool Dockers, Anteus Graphics, Liverpool 1996 (144 Kensington, Liverpool L7 8XE).

agency. The MDHC and union paid financial consultants (KPMG) to devise a specific plan for an agency which could re-employ some dockers on 'self-employed', insecure terms. This plan was rejected by the workers because it would further institutionalise and legitimise casualisation, with the TGWU acting as a sponsor.

In spite of substantial support, both nationwide and internationally, by late 1997 the sacked dockers were unable to make further headway and were suffering acute financial difficulties. A further rebuff came in December 1997, when the TGWU leadership refused to support their solidarity call to the International Transport Workers' Federation. In early 1998 they accepted a settlement, with redundancy payments similar to those which the MDHC had offered much earlier.

Within Britain, solidarity efforts were co-ordinated by the London Support Group for the Liverpool Dockers, which organised national demonstrations and other activities. The Liverpool dockers attracted widespread support from direct-action movements, for several reasons. They were challenging the anti-solidarity laws, pursuing their struggle independently of trade union officials, and had previously campaigned to prevent the import of toxic waste. 'Reclaim the Streets' (RTS) mobilised in support of the dockers on a number of occasions. And in January 1997, when dockers at ports worldwide were blocking or delaying ships from Liverpool, Greenpeace activists occupied a crane in the Liverpool port, highlighting the shipments of Monsanto's genetically modified soybeans arriving in the UK and Europe.

At marches and other solidarity events, trade unions were represented mainly by members with no job or whose jobs were relatively low-paid and insecure. For example, heading the People's March for Social Justice in April 1997 were groups of sacked workers from the Liverpool docks, Hillingdon Hospital, Magnet Kitchens, etc. The best supported trade union banners were those of Turkish or Kurdish workers' branches, from poorly paid sectors such as the garment industry. For this network of ex-workers and precariously-employed people, their political identity came more from solidarity activity than from any actual 'employment' or 'dignity of work'.

During their dispute, the sacked dockers expressed different visions of what was possible or desirable in the future of work. According to the shop stewards, management needs a 'professional' labour force, which in the case of the Liverpool docks could only be provided by experienced (i.e. sacked) dockers. This argument defends the jobs which had been fought for, so that secure jobs may be handed on to future generations. At the same time, some suggested a more open-ended future: 'Not many human beings would choose freely to spend their lives in the tumult of meaningless, unfulfilling and alienated work … The struggle of the dockers in Liverpool is not to maintain the past but to protect the future', according to shop steward Mike Carden. And at a public meeting where dockers' leaders were drawing lessons from the dispute, one shop steward questioned whether it made sense to demand 'the right to work' in a period when capitalism could no longer provide the sorts of industrial jobs on which the labour movement had been built.

Future strategies?

European integration has been bound up with agendas for flexibilising labour in order to intensify its exploitation. Neoliberalism seeks to maximise the labour supply for capital, rather than create jobs which accommodate workers' needs for income, dignity and security. Regardless of the various statutory and policy changes involved, however, their material effects will depend upon the power of capitalism to impose work discipline, and upon the counter-power to resist. For that reason, it is important to analyse neoliberal strategies and counter-strategies. What can be learned from the UK experience for Europe-wide struggles?

As a neoliberal vanguard, the UK has provided a Europe-wide impetus and model for flexploitation. Neoliberal strategies have weakened employment security, worker solidarity and the shop-steward organisations which formerly defended workers' autonomy from capitalist work discipline. Moreover, some UK trade unions have internalised this agenda; even when the leadership is left-wing, they have used anti-solidarity legislation to isolate those who resist, for the sake of partnership with management.

As jobs become flexibilised, so do the unemployed. Workfare-type schemes blur the distinction between employment and unemployment. Even more public money is spent to 'train' and police the unemployed. These pressures undermine worker solidarity and the capacity to resist flexibilisation, especially when trade unions collude in such schemes.

Although sacked workers demand reinstatement on dignified terms, they seek 'jobs' of a sort which have been abolished. In particular the Liverpool dockers fought to preserve jobs that appeared as community assets - jobs with security, pride, and some degree of workers' autonomy established through shop steward power. Paradoxically, in pursuing such demands, they create dignified political work which they do unpaid, whilst lacking an adequate political language to describe it.

Their resistance has catalysed and attracted new activist networks. Many such people alternate between precarity and unemployment, often rejecting or de-prioritising paid capitalist work in their lives. By contrast to the traditional left demand for 'full employment', they promote a vision of collective activity (paid or unpaid) necessary to meet social needs. Many would argue that everyone has *too much* capitalist work, e.g. through overtime, workfare schemes, training courses to obtain qualifications, etc. As an international gathering stated, 'dignity is taken away from us when the capitalist work machine uses us for its purposes'.[13]

The threat of boundless capitalist work has been intensified by the significant shift in employment and welfare policy in the UK in particular. State expenditure is redirected to subsidise insecure, low-paid work - aimed not only at the 'unemployed', but potentially at anyone who suffers from 'social exclusion'. Through various carrots and sticks, the state attempts to draw mothers of young children, people with disabilities and the early-retired back into the labour force for capital - often at the expense of parenting, rest and recuperation. Some feminist agendas (more childcare provision, more financial independence for women) are easily co-opted into this labour maximisation discourse, while neoliberal policies fail to address the significant gender gap in pay.

As the neoliberal project seeks to maximise the labour supply for capital, traditional left demands for 'full employment' can fall into a trap. Such demands inadvertently accommodate the neoliberal agenda of relentless work discipline, defining 'employment' as any work - however badly paid, insecure or socially meaningless. By characterising casual employment and even workfare as 'jobs',

---

13. *Reports from the Second Intercontinental Encuentro For Humanity Against Neoliberalism*: 'Introduction', Massimo de Angelis; Report from mesa 1a&b; Declaration of El Indiana, *Capital & Class* 65, 1998; also at http://www.geocities.com/CapitolHill/3849/report_mesa1a1b.html.

trade unions treat any job as a gift from capital, rather than opposing exploitation as the major issue.

All those tensions arose in the European Marches 'against unemployment, precarity and social exclusion'. The campaign opposed workfare-type schemes, while leaving vague the terms for social inclusion. On the one hand, its demands for 'full employment' were important for obtaining trade union support. On the other hand, its demands for a 'guaranteed minimum income' were important for unemployed groups.

Unemployed activists eventually pushed the EuroMarch campaign to reject the 'full employment' slogan, on the grounds that it could only mean an 'over-full employment of low-paid precarious jobs'. Moreover, by demanding a guaranteed minimum income, the campaign linked this with the need for free collective provision of basic services, health, education, etc.

If a movement is going to expand such efforts, then a new political language is needed to express aspirations for different ways of living and working. Such efforts depend on the answers to a strategic question: on what collective basis do we oppose flexploitation, link the various resistances, appropriate resources for people's needs, and create our own dignified work?

The first version of this essay was written by the authors with other members of For Humanity Against Neo-liberalism (fHUMAN), London Committee. It was presented at the Second Intercontinental Encuentro For Humanity Against Neoliberalism in August 1997, in a workshop entitled 'Work & Creating a Life with Dignity' (Encuentro 1998). The original essay has been revised to locate and update the UK analysis within its European context.

Further background material

Aufheben (2000) *Stop the Clock! Critiques of the New Social Workhouse*, Aufheben c/o Brighton & Hove Unemployed Workers Centre, aufheben99@yahoo.co.uk, http://lists.village.Virginia.EDU/~spoons/aut_html/auf1edit.htm

Do or Die (1999) 'Globalisation: origins-history-analysis-resistance', *Do or Die* 8: 35-54, available at http://www.eco-action.org/dod, or at http://www.freespeech.org/mayday2k/readings.htm

Gray, A. (1995) 'Flexibilisation of labour and the attack on workers' living standards', *Common Sense* 18: 12-32, Edinburgh CSE, http://www.geocities.com/CapitolHill/3843/gray1.html; postscript is available on http://www.geocities.com/CapitolHill/3843/gray2.html

Gray, A. (1998) 'New Labour - new labour discipline', *Capital & Class* 65: 1-8. For *Capital & Class* in general see http://www.cseweb.org.uk

King, D. and Wickham-Jones, M. (1999) 'From Clinton to Blair: the Democratic (Party) Origins of Welfare to Work', *Political Quarterly* 70(1): 62-74; also in M. Powell, ed., *New Labour, New Welfare State?*, Cambridge: Polity.

McIlroy, J. (2000) 'New Labour, New Unions, New Left', *Capital & Class* 71: 11-45.

Mathers, A. (1999) 'EuroMarch: struggle for a social Europe', *Capital & Class* 68: 15-19.

Mathers, A. and Taylor, G. (2000) 'Europe-wide struggles against neoliberalism', paper presented at Conference of Socialist Economists, http://www.cseweb.org.uk, see under Conference 2000.

Pilger, J. (1998) 'The dockers', in J. Pilger, *Hidden Agendas*, London: Vintage, pp334-58.

Siebert, R. (2000) 'Making Europe work: the struggle to cut the workweek', *Capital & Class* 71: 1-10.

What is to be done about boys?

Linda McDowell

Linda McDowell looks at some of the myths about young working-class men.

I had arranged to meet Darren in a pub on the edge of a local authority estate in Sheffield, but he'd been banned the evening before for using foul and aggressive language; so instead we found ourselves in a windswept car park wondering where else to go and talk on a dark late November evening. Darren was not much past 16 that autumn, a tall, well-built youth who didn't say a great deal, but what he did was carefully considered. I had come to Sheffield to talk to him and some of his friends, who were among a group of young school leavers from a 'failing' school.[1] I wanted to find out whether current media images of bolshy lads, outperformed at school by girls, competing for jobs in the 'feminised' service sector and worried about their masculine identity, had any resonance with young men in the deindustrialising city of Sheffield. Earlier in the year I had also talked to a similar group in Cambridge where service work had long dominated the

1. I talked to ten young white men from working-class backgrounds living on local authority estates in Cambridge, and thirteen in Sheffield. All the young men were aged 15 or 16 and in the last term of compulsory schooling when I first talked to them in the early summer of 1999. I met to them twice more over the next year, asking them about their hopes and aspirations, their job prospects, their view of their 'local community' and neighbourhood as well as about their everyday lives.

local economy.

As we move into the twenty-first century, it has begun to seem as if the rhetoric of gender inequality has been reversed - increasingly the problems of inequity and under-achievement seem to be those of young men. There are three strands to the argument. The first area where boys are represented as under-achievers, even failures, is in school leaving exams. In the last few years, each August when the GCSE results are published, the relative failure of boys compared to girls is headline news. In fact the gender gap is small - less that 10 per cent - and a growing number of school leavers of both sexes are achieving good results (defined as at least five GCSEs at grade C or above). Thus, in 2001 about 50 per cent of the age cohort reached this level of attainment, compared to just under 25 per cent fifteen years earlier. The problem of low attainment is not a gender issue per se, but rather one of connections between gender, class and ethnicity. It is working-class boys and boys of African-Caribbean origins who continue to perform poorly, not boys in general. Middle-class youths attending 'good' schools continue to gain excellent results and are moving into post-compulsory education in increasing numbers.

The reasons for the poor performance of some working-class boys, instead of being located in an explanation that emphasises low expectations, poverty or racism, are instead commonly found in the second strand of current debates about the 'problem with boys'. These young men are not reaching their potential at school because they are 'lads' or 'yobs', only interested in having a good time and disturbing the peace of more respectable citizens in the process. The Labour government argues that the yobbish culture on the football terrace and public spaces coincides with the 'laddish' culture of schools, which was identified in 1998 by Stephen Byers (then a junior minister in the Department of Education and Employment) as the main cause of boy's underachievement. Similar comments about 'lads', and about the absence of male role models for failing boys, were also made in the following years by David Blunkett. Other apparent culprits variously include feminist teachers and men's magazines, and in 2000 the debate was given a new twist by sociologist Tony Sewell, himself Black British, arguing that the materialist emphasis in black youth culture on style and appearance is a key part of the explanation for boys' low achievement rates (*Independent* 18.8.00).

The class, as well as racialised, connotations of these debates about yobs and lads are clear. When Tony Blair, in the inappropriate context of an address in Germany in summer 2000, made his curious pronouncement that in future thugs, yobs and hooligans who disrupted the peace of Britain's streets through their drunken and disorderly behaviour would be summarily marched to cash points to pay on-the-spot fines, he probably little imagined that just three weeks later his own son, then aged 16 and celebrating the end of compulsory schooling, would be found face-down, drunk and incapable, in a London gutter. Hooligans are not, in the popular imagination, responsible middle-class schoolboys but working class 'yobs'. But, as Jack Straw also had cause to rue, this assumption that it's other people's kids who make trouble, get pissed, smoke dope or worse, is not necessarily true.

Despite these personal challenges, Labour policy pronouncements continued to firmly reflect the view that it was young working-class men who were out of control. During the week in which his son was arrested Blair had made several policy pronouncements about youth 'justice', in part spurred by the spectacle of British soccer supporters at European cup matches. In an article headed 'Policing Yob Culture' (*Guardian* 3.7.00), Tony Blair was reported as being on a law and order kick: 'After his weekend speech urging on the spot fines for drunken, noisy, loutish and anti-social behaviour, he is now proposing new police fines or 48-hour closure orders on rowdy pubs' (p4); such pubs were referred to by the PM as 'thug pubs'. Meanwhile, the aim of reducing 'disorderly' behaviour had been written into a Home Office Crime Reduction Strategy, and Jack Straw, then Home Office Minister, on 3 July announced 'zero-tolerance' 'anti-social behaviour orders', under which the courts had new powers to jail anyone who was persistently disorderly but not convicted of a specific crime. As Ros Coward (*Guardian* 4.7.00) noted, not only was the rhetoric emotive and Blair's language particularly florid, but it dishonestly conflated delinquent behaviour with more serious problems of violent crime. It was, Coward suggested, 'bogeyman politics, spinning working-class men as hate figures'.

In January 2001, this conflation was even more evident when headlines greeting the new Criminal Justice Bill argued that it gave 'More clout for police in tackling murders and drunken yobs' (*Guardian* 20.1.01), in a ludicrous juxtaposition of problems of a significantly different magnitude. In this bill, new powers were outlined to introduce fixed penalty fines for drunken and disorderly behaviour, being drunk and incapable, and using threatening words. Later in the year, in August 2001, it was announced that the hitherto-unused powers given to local authorities in 1998 to introduce curfews between 10pm and 6am for the under 11s were to be extended. The police, as well as local authorities, would be able to apply for curfew orders for under-16s who made a nuisance of themselves. The Home Office Minister Beverley Hughes, who made the announcement in the Commons, noted, 'When people find they have had their car sprayed, or their windows broken in, those are the issues that make life very difficult for people living on

'older forms of acceptable "macho" behaviour are now a positive disadvantage in the labour market'

some of our neighbourhood estates'. She added that the curfews would 'help the local community to feel empowered to take responsibility for their own children' (*Guardian* 2.8.01). Her careful use of the euphemisms 'neighbourhood estates' and 'local community' fails to disguise the class-specific nature of the measure. It is working-class rather than middle-class parents who will have to keep their teenagers penned up on summer evenings, if curfew orders are ever implemented, and it is working-class kids on council estates who are assumed to cause all the trouble in the first place.

The third strand to the arguments about the growing 'problem with boys' lies in looking at the effects of economic restructuring, especially the decline of manufacturing and the growing concentration of employment in poorly-paid, bottom end service sector jobs. Twenty-five years ago working-class men who left school as soon as they could were able to find reasonably secure and relatively well-paid work in the manufacturing sector. Today their sons are more likely to have to look for work in the service sector, where casualised and insecure work is poorly remunerated, especially for young workers, who are a significant part of the labour force in catering, fast food and the retail sector. Under 18s are excluded from the provisions of minimum wage legislation and 18-21 year olds are eligible only for the youth rate. Further, work in the service sector demands a particular sort of embodied performance in which clean and well-presented employees have to provide a polite and deferential service. Older forms of acceptable 'macho' behaviour among working-class men, which used to be a key feature of male manual employment, as well as contemporary 'laddish', aggressive, or 'in yer face' versions of masculinity, are now a positive disadvantage in the labour market, where self presentation, punctuality, attitude, and demeanour towards customers and superiors, are important. Attributes such as deference and docility, more commonly associated with socially constructed views of femininity, are now the most highly valued skills in the bottom end service sector jobs. If male socialisation in schools and in the locality continues to emphasise traditional male ways of doing things, young men may find themselves increasingly excluded from the only labour market opportunities open to them. The youth labour market is also especially susceptible to economic downturns, and the association between urban unrest in British cities in 1981, 1991 and 2001, and high rates of unemployment among young men, especially in inner London and in deindustrialising cities in the north, is noticeable.

The combination of these educational and economic changes has led many commentators to identity a crisis of masculinity among young men. But what do young men themselves think of this idea? Are male school leavers increasingly disadvantaged in the service sector? And is the version of laddish masculinity presented in policy debates the only option open to them in the transition from school to adult worker? These were the sorts of questions I explored with Darren and his friends. What they told me both confirmed and challenged current views of working-class 'lads'. On some occasions and in some parts of their daily life they conformed to stereotypical views of lad or yob behaviour, but most of them also held down jobs and had clear ideas about masculine responsibilities. What saddened me was the extent to which these youths were aware of, and had internalised, majority views of themselves as 'a waste of space' (Chris, Cambridge), despite, as I show below, their commitment to 'traditional' values such as the work ethic and domestic responsibility. All 23 of the young men I interviewed may have accepted their designation as a 'lad', but they explicitly rejected the label 'yob', drawing a clear line between 'enjoying yourself' and 'going too far'. 'I may get drunk but I don't go out looking for trouble' (Darren, Sheffield). I have chosen two youths - almost at random but reasonably representative - to speak for their cohort.

Darren left school just after Easter without sitting any exams and had had two jobs over the year in which I got to know him. He hated school, not persuaded of the values of education, but also resentful of how the predominantly middle-class teachers had labelled him as disruptive: 'You know once you have got a name, they sort of treat you reet differently from other people in the class. It's how they talk to you, like. "It's him again. It's that Darren again". I feel like I've got a sign on me head saying I've done summat wrong'. Darren was identified by the school as a low achiever and sent on a part-time release scheme to a local college, 'to do painting, decorating, construction, woodwork, all that stuff', because, as he told me, 'I'm not very brainy and that and teachers expect you to do more stuff than you can'. Consequently, in years 10 and 11, 'I just used to wag it [play truant] most of the time'. And yet he also told me that when he left school, he regretted giving up German. This was the one subject he had enjoyed and felt he might do reasonably well in, because 'we have individual lessons for it, you know, like for people who didn't used to come to school, you have individual lessons. There's only abht seven in't class. Teacher's all reet'.

The local estate, built between the 1930s and 1950s, where Darren lived with his parents and older brother, was troubled by many of the issues identified by Beverley Hughes: vandalism, graffiti, car thefts and joy riding. Darren explained that he didn't get involved, although he had been hanging around with some of the older boys involved and had been cautioned for petty theft as: 'me Dad told me if he sees me with them I'm grounded' - an indication that perhaps the Labour curfew would find favour in some areas. When I asked him if his parents were strict his answer was revealing. 'No, they are just like normal parents, like. They want - they don't want coppers coming to the house all the time and that, nowt like that': visits that working-class parents in the area found all too common.

I asked Darren whether he thought most young men of his acquaintance would be seen as yobs, as the sort of men whose behaviour Blair was anxious to change. As already noted, Darren had been banned from the local pub for using foul language; and for him, as for many of his peers, drinking was a key part of a Friday night out with the lads: 'I'll drink five or six pints if I go to a pub; eight or nine if I go clubbing. I go out with £40 on a Friday and a Saturday, mebbe a bit more on Saturdays'. But he was absolutely clear that although he might get drunk, he was never incapable and nor would he go out looking for trouble. 'I know what I am doing. I like enjoying meself on weekend, but I don't drink on the streets; just go out to the pubs and have a laff with some of me mates. I don't cause no trouble or owt'. And later he elaborated: 'I'm just a lad - someone who doesn't cause trouble but who's sociable and likes a laugh'. For more sober citizens meeting Darren with six of seven of his friends after they'd drunk nine pints, the distinction between a lad and a yob might seem rather academic. However, as a youth worker in Toxteth told Hilary Wainwright, 'they [young people] appear more intimidating than they are'(see *Soundings* 18).

Darren might look intimidating and sometimes get drunk, but he was also a hard worker, who didn't drink to anything like the same extent on weekdays as he did at the weekend. When I talked to him for the third time, he had a job as an assistant to a fibre glass mould-maker and was learning how to laminate. Before that he'd worked on an industrial site on a concrete crushing machine but had been made redundant. He had been out of work for a few weeks but he 'didn't bother with the dole or that'. Darren was committed to the values of work, determined to 'make a go of it', describing himself as 'a reliable worker'. He lived at home with his parents, contributing £15 a week for his food. He spoke fondly of his family, especially his father: 'He does a lot of things for other people, like. See, he's a mechanic and if people want to buy a car, he like go and have a look for 'em like before they buy it, helpin' them like, and he doesn't charge em or owt; he just does it for a favour'. It was clear too that Darren had strong views about his local area, where he said he intended to remain. 'Well, it used to be a quiet place but it in't no more, like there's all trouble and that. Fighting, smashed windows and cars getting nicked, all that sort of stuff. Police don't do much, just patrol area every so often, that's it. And there's loads of groups of people that hangs about the shops with beers and that. Just daft. Out in cold weather stood on street corners … They used to be up at youth club. But now they've stopped it so there's nowhere else they can go'. Notice that Darren does not include himself among these young people, being too busy with 'me job and that'.

Another of my interviewees, Wayne, lives in Cambridge, on a more recently built estate on the outskirts of the city. When he is out on the town on a Friday night, he too might seem to personify the 'yob' that the Labour Cabinet is so anxious about. In Wayne's case, his attitudes are more troublesome than those of the somewhat phlegmatic but reliable Darren. Wayne was also categorised as a low achiever at his school and like Darren he was a reluctant school attender. Wayne also felt that he, and in this case a small group of his friends, caught the blame for all sorts of incidents. 'Well, if something happens at school like, like a child got stoned [stones thrown in the playground], or like chopped up [pushed in the corridors], like the teacher would say "look, it's, it's the boys again, they done it again, ent they?"' But, he continued, on reflection, 'We're more mature now, we just don't bother. We like to help 'em if they're getting picked on, you see. Cuz we're top of the school, we can't just walk down the corridor pushin' them over and punchin' them'. Intimidation may have still played a part though, as Wayne added, 'Well, I think it's quite cool actually. Walkin' down the corridor and they all just move out of the way'.

Wayne's behaviour and attitudes out of school also seemed to parallel Darren's. Wayne drew a clear line between what he regarded as semi-criminal acts of little significance and 'real trouble'. 'Well, we only ever mucked about. In car parks [of a shopping centre] at night, like. We used to muck about with the security guard, like walk past him and swear at him or something. We nicked hub-caps off the wheels too. We used to take them away but it's not really worth it now. We used to like just take them and smash them up, just for the fun of it'. He paused and, smiling engagingly, said 'Sound like a right old thug, don't I?' And, like generations of American teenagers before him, Wayne also told me, 'we hang about the centre of town. Jamie's got a really nice car, and he's done it up real nice and all the birds stare at it, so we go over there and he sits in it revving it up and then, and then, then a few of his other mates come over and their cars and they like race around the market square. I know you are not supposed to do that, but they just do it anyway'.

W hen he left school, Wayne had initially intended to go straight to work but found it difficult to find something suitable for a 16-year-old. He went to the local job centre where he was advised to consider the modern apprenticeship scheme. He made a successful application to a local building firm and he started in July, sponsored by the firm for periods of block release at the local Further Education College to study for a GNVQ (starting at level 1). Like Darren, he was a determined worker, attending regularly and reliably, despite having to get up extremely early on the morning when he was working away from Cambridge. His GCSE results had been poor (grade D was his highest achievement) and so he found college hard work: 'at college I don't like the writing side of it. I'd rather be doing more practical stuff and that'. And like Darren he seemed to have a sadly clear-sighted view of his own abilities 'I knew I weren't going to get As, Bs, or Cs and anything like that 'cos I know I ain't no good'; but, he continued, 'I'll stick at this [his apprenticeship]. I always used to muck about at school, but now I'm sorted; if you know what you are doing it's all right'. Wayne was earning £100 a week in May 2000, from which he gave his mother £20. 'Well, that includes my water and stuff and I get free use of the telephone and I get television and stuff, so I think that's all right, isn't it?' And later he said, 'I give it them on a Thursday when I get paid and then I borrow it back at the weekend!'

Despite looking younger than Darren, Wayne was also a keen Friday and Saturday night drinker and clubber, although he avoided going drinking on Sundays and during the week as he had to get up for work the next morning. He drinks 'every Friday night, it's a regular thing', sometimes in pubs and sometimes taking lager from the off-licence to a friend's house. 'I am not really old enough to drink, but I can get served anyway. I drink nine bottles, but it's not too bad as it's usually only one night a week'. He told me that he had tried soft drugs but preferred to drink, 'except for the problem of having to pee every five minutes'. When he goes clubbing, he sometimes gets into fights, often deliberately, on his own admission, but he always tries to stay out of serious trouble. He had never been arrested and described himself as a 'Jack the lad', out for having fun, meeting girls but not looking for trouble.

Wayne was one of the most style-conscious of the 23 young men, with a different haircut each time I saw him, dyed, gelled, long strands over a short undercut: 'I don't like to wear a hard hat at work cos it mucks me hair up'. He wore chains and rings - 'I take me rings off if I am going to hit someone. I don't want to cut me hands up' - and was unthinkingly sexist. And yet he was charming, courteous and thoughtful and, like Darren, fond of his parents and anxious about the decline of his local neighbourhood. For both of them work was the central element of their lives and they described to me in great detail the specifics of their daily tasks, how to lay bricks, how to sort scrap from reusable materials, how long laminating takes on different materials, as well as details of their working lives, including the comments and jokes made by their work mates. They recognised their luck in getting work that was regular and in Darren's case would lead to a good trade.

Most of the other school leavers to whom I spoke worked in service sector jobs, where the hours were irregular and the pay poorer. Most of them had casual or temporary employment without contracts or employment-related benefits such as holiday entitlement. Catering, cleaning and working in the retail sector were common jobs, in which, as Simon in Cambridge said, 'the work is horrible but at least I am working and getting paid'. In Sheffield McDonalds was a significant employer of school leavers - four of the thirteen youths I interviewed worked there. And although, as Richard told me, 'it's mindless work and it's not easy either', like his peers, he was determined to stick to it until he could find something better.

These young men are not mindless vandals or thugs, but carefully calculating, rational young people, who have worked out what seem to them to be acceptable limits of laddish behaviour in their social lives - limits that are compatible with regular labour market participation and responsibility to their parents. Their lives and future opportunities are no doubt circumscribed, limited by their lack of educational achievement and low incomes, and the type of work which they were doing as school leavers was often dull and repetitive. But even the most basic of entry-level employment depends on skills which deserve greater recognition. These youths were developing time discipline, learning to use tills, and developing their capacity to engage in personal interactions with customers and co-workers. As Katherine Newman, in her splendid study of working in fast food outlets in New York, insisted, these sort of low income and casualised employees deserve respect, not denigration.[2] In Britain, policies to widen young workers' horizons, to extend training opportunities and construct pathways between low income entry-level positions and more permanent, better paid work, as well as new initiatives to encourage them to remain in or return to education, would have a great deal more to offer the young men to whom I talked than punitive actions to restrict their impact in and on the public. At present, workfare policies such as the New Deal focus almost solely on labour supply measures and pay insufficient attention to the type of work and conditions of employment, let alone to job creation programmes that should be an essential part of improving the life chances of that minority of young men who still leave school at the first

---

2. K. Newman, *No Shame in my Game: the working poor in the inner city*, Vintage Books and Russell Sage Foundation, New York 1999.

opportunity. Fining them £100 for drinking, when most estates have almost no alternative leisure facilities for young people (as was the case in both cities in my research) is an inadequate response to the 'problem with boys'.

The interviews with young men in Cambridge and Sheffield were funded by the Joseph Rowntree Foundation as part of their Youth Programme. I am extremely grateful for their support.

London diaries

Bronislaw Malinowski, Grazyna Kubica

Grazyna Kubica *compares notes with Malinowski.*

September 1913

It is only after the passage of two years that I have found myself alone again and can reckon the accounts of the time past and fortify myself for the future. My problem currently lies, above all, in work technique and an economy of physical strength. My powers are very limited while my desires of all manner and type immeasurably animated. I have managed to limit them in various points and thus relieve myself of unnecessary expenditure of energy. Nonetheless, inasmuch as I know my strength, I am unable to lead them to harmony with my goals, and thus my work technique, as well as the ratio of my plans to things completed, is rather piteous. The thing is to think over the events of the past months and draw conclusions for the future.

1 February 1999

London - The very name forces one to straighten up and bravely face the world. Will be here for two weeks, sitting in the archives over M's diaries, and in the evenings write mine. This isn't some diary disease, but a literature which saves. I'll also take my first photographic self-portrait. This will be a liminally suspended time, an important moment, a turning point.

September 1913

Arrival in London has undoubtedly started a new phase in my life. Completely new surroundings. New people, and a new way of working in the library; independent work with the concrete thought of publication. Especially since it is all in England, about which I have long dreamed and to which I referred in a quite extraordinary way, acting under strong prestige. Above all, however, a change in my home life. For the first time for a long time, I have lived under circumstances completely corresponding to marriage. Each night I returned home, was expected. All of this very strongly colours life. Arrival full of disquiet, expectation and that shivering uncertainty which always precedes contact with a new thing which is to be a part of my existence in the future. In this Home an interesting *Stimmung*, everything is 'English', exaggerated apperception of all details through this general concept.

2 February 1999

Rain falls, but it's relatively warm. I'm walking a bit faster, don't pause at the shop windows, don't stare, don't reflect. From Byng Place I take a shortcut through London University campus, cross Russell Square diagonally, and then along Southampton Row to Holborn and then to Kingsway. In a small cafe I drink an espresso standing, turn into Portugal Street and go to the School [LSE]. Recall my last being here over ten years ago, lunch eaten on the terrace, white chairs, blinding sun, Maurice Bloch, conversations with him, seminar, controversial subjects. That stay of mine, mainly in Oxford on the invitation of St John's College, but also later in London, was made possible due to my illegal underground contact with the Jagiellonian Trust. This was an archetypal journey to the sources of knowledge, mainly thanks to Edwin Ardener and Shirley, with whom I communicated on some deeper level, though often I did not understand particular phrases of their personal language. To my great surprise I realised that I was made for college life, that I felt like a fish in water there, that I didn't have any reservations or complexes, which I had feared a bit, especially considering the unrefined communism with which I had arrived and the Lutheran-peasant upbringing I had taken from my home. Remember Sir Raymond making fun of his knighthood, lunch in his club. Visit in Cambridge with Ernest Gellner, dinner at King's College (some guy is proudly wearing an anarchistically pink bow tie). Day spent at Jerzy Slawomir's, Helena Wayne-Malinowska's Russet Cottage, wondrous incarnation of the address so many times written down by me. In London at Tom's, his bikes, together at Jeane La Fontaine's and also at Patrick's, at Dennis O'Keeffe's, at Scruton's. Mrs Dobroczynska and the ghastly monotony of the houses in Wimbledon. The agreeable air on the hills of Hornsey, when I was coming back from Bishop Fierla's, who was with my grandfather in a concentration camp, and was present at his death. The bishop's nice house. Was my grandfather like him? How would he act towards me?

Little wagon, the fields lightly shrouded in fog, Chatham and the black waters of the reservoir with armoured ships, Canterbury, England, and the arrival in London; the bridge. There is no one at Victoria. Night. I take the bus on Finsborough St. Rain starts to fall. I'm carrying my letters. Don't have money, desperate situation. Go to Star St. Then Saville St. Then to Ken Walk. On the second day I'm a bit out of sorts. N in a red dress, we find an apartment at 16 Fitzroy St. Then a walk. Lunch at Shearns. East[er] holidays. Visit at Auntie's. Quarrel (about the Messiah).

I can say that my life that spring comprises two parts: British Mus[eum] and the acquaintances and relationships which group around that. And Saville Street. Brit[ish] Mus[eum] Reading Room, I show it my reverence. Some special value of knowledge that one acquires there. From the beginning I sit at D2. First acquaintance with Spearman. He speaks of Rivers; I read Todas, Schurtz. Work on *Altersklassen*. Kuorter and I go to Cambridge. Riv[ers] and Haddon. The honeymoon of my ardour for England. In Cambr[idge], I go in the evening with K to see Riv[ers]; moonlit night; the courtyard of St John's looks like a fairy-tale; in a high, dark room, a thin man; give him a few compliments about Todas and begin to talk with him about magic & economy. The next day I read *Reports*; go for lunch to his house. Haddon. Then we visit the College. The next day we go to Hadd[on]. The whole afternoon Miss Marreco & the priest speak of S[outh] Afr[ica], I'm delighted. With Hadd[on]. Set a date that I'll go to Forest Hill on Saturday. I return, she meets me at Kings Cross, pleasant afternoon. Later I was with Haddon at For[est] Hill. Read Frobenius and others, Hutton Webster, Morgan, too. Tarnowski. Westermarck introduces me to Wheeler, seminar (Austey). Visit at Mr Koch's; read Lévy Bruehl during it. That stay in Midhurst and reading that book were nearly the only moment of real, cognitive fertility. Then with N to the Isle of Wight. Pretty house facing the sea. Moonlit night. Walk on the dangerous undercliff near the hospital towards St Catherine's. Strong fatigue, drowsiness. Aha, one more thing! 'Death of the King' on the day in which I leave for Koch's. Then, before the holidays we go to the I[sle] o[f] W[ight]. N returns for a funeral, I stay until Friday. On the I[sle] o[f] W[ight], make a plan for my paper to be read at Westermarck's and write it. Under the influence of what Riv[ers] told me and what I have understood from Levy Bruehl, I am beginning to think about and deal with classes and their attitude towards family.

Yes, real England where moderate order is connected with a fundamental permanence of issues and things. One could have a justifiable certainty that if on one floor of some public building there is only a men's toilet, then on the next there will be a women's. You go one floor higher and there it is! And sinks have two faucets: warm and cold.

The building of the School [LSE]. The main cafeteria. A crowd of black-haired young people of both sexes, more or less tawny-skinned. Blondes, the brown-haired and red-haired are an insignificant minority. Everyone has a cellular phone, over the clamour of conversations, piercing screeches arise. It is irritating to see such a huge number of people, all, most unexpectedly, extraordinarily devoted to life: they talk, charm and delight one another, discuss, tell tales, flirt, read aloud, point to something in the newspaper, and all the while bite, drink, smoke (but only in the segregated section). The most irritating are naturally the female students. All are very pretty and moderately made up.

In this dough of effervescent youth are scattered, like raisins (but maybe like worms) the elderly: grey-haired, bald, wrinkled, tired, and, if younger, then ugly, all deep in thought, tired, accustomed to going about their business over and beyond this bubbling youth. But actually, why have they come here, and not a floor higher to the Senior Common Room Cafeteria? They wear grey suits or sports jackets, but some allow themselves the luxury of a sweater and jeans (the humanities?). They sit by themselves or a few to a group. They converse, even gesticulate, but they are sad (perhaps they simply don't smile), but the saddest are the female scholars. They wear bland clothing, have wrinkles, uncared for hair, and are very few to be seen.

The sixth floor of the main building of LSE, the room next to the secretariat: the Friday anthropology seminar. The person convening it must have had at least one parent who was a poet because her name is - Fenella Canell.

This time the speaker is a long-haired (pony-tailed), bearded, young Englishman who speaks of the manners of self-identification of various groups of Pygmies in the Congo. He sits at a large, oval table, together with the convenor and others working in the institute. The rest (doctoral students), inasmuch as there is room, sit on chairs, crowded along the walls, and the bookshelves, and then they sit wherever possible - on the floor.

There are no suits (except for mine). In the best case there is a suit coat (no tie) or a jacket. Sweaters and jeans dominate. Still, some of the women dress in a more elegant manner. Across from me sits an intriguingly beautiful Turkish(?) woman: black pants, a dark, close-fitting blouse, smoothly brushed hair tied in a *tight bun, big eyes, lightly made-up, very (perhaps too) prominent lips coated by something nearly indiscernible. She behaves a bit flirtatiously (rare).*

The guy who is talking cites his African interlocutors, also using shouts, cries, and grumbles, etc. This meets with the approving laughter of the gathered (especially the women).

Around the table sit only white people, on the chairs there is a complete mixture. Across from me from the left are a Chinese woman, a white woman, a Greek woman, a black man, a red-headed woman, the pretty Turkish woman, a southern European, a white man (horridly muddied shoes), white woman, white man (head shaved), etc. (Of course, these are my completely unjustified presumptions drawn from completely unjustified premises, to define someone's identity on the basis of their external appearance.)

The handsome speaker almost shouts when he cites his Pygmies. Not everyone is listening carefully, but when he shouts his quotes they all wake up.

Behind the table men dominate (7:5), on the seats women (15:11). Next to a sticker reading 'No smoking' there is a computer printed note: 'Absolutely No Smoking At Any Time'. Obviously in England there is some conviction that warnings forbidding something are directed at only some categories of people (students, guests), and not for others (employees, residents).

The end. Rustling. What we heard was 'tremendously entertaining, great fun'. The speaker explains that war, although it has not reached them as yet, has disturbed the delicate order of relationships between the groups under discussion. Wages are not paid out so everyone is dependent upon corruption. The convenor surveys the room for those wanting to take part in the discussion. The women anthropologists seem mostly not to use make-up. Only the prettiest ones do. Nearly everyone behind the table and the seated men ask questions. The young women sit quietly. The convenor: 'It was an extremely interesting discussion', which will be continued in the bar where everyone is invited.

I buy myself a small Guinness and wait for her. When she arrives, a game of 'hot potato' begins: I have to introduce myself, briefly state what I am doing and then - 'please meet my colleague' - and I have to introduce myself again to the next person. This lasts until I come across someone who is truly interested in what I do, or will at least pretend to be so out of respect for my femininity, or I'll finally say something intelligent enough that it will go beyond normal conversation and then they will start talking with me normally.

Saville St, narrow, little street so filthy that it beats all records within the entire quarter, and indisputably Jewish. Mornings the apartment reeked of smoke and the odour of fried fat. Children hollered mercilessly on the street all day long, that is, unless a hurdy-gurdy or other instrument of torture wasn't to be heard over them. One entered through glass doors, with one pane that was always being broken by the young Kohn.

A small foyer, toilet and kitchen. Then a dining room & sitting room. There we ate breakfast and dinner together. For breakfast usually jam, tea & porridge. For dinner salad and cold meat. Then roast. Red wine (Australian burgundy). On Fitzroy St I slept only twice, once when N was ill and Mr Wah was guarding the door, and the second time when I was coming home from somewhere very late. I don't remember the details of this life in historical order any more. Morning, hard to get up. Then exercises and washing. Breakfast. Go through F[itzroy] St so as to pick up letters. The view of the street in green and the trees on the square. I move quickly and as if fearfully down the steps. Change my shoes and take the letters. In N's black leather bag I carry papers. I go through Tottenham Ct. Rd, through Store Street or straight towards Bedford Sq[uare] to the Br[itish] Mus[eum].

5 February 1999

I am living in the Quaker Guest House (because it is inexpensive and close). Quakers here appear in the form of a few persons of undefined competencies. There are meditation rooms here in which meetings sometimes take place of only older women (excepting the leader). Besides that, this house does not differ in any way from an ordinary, inexpensive hotel. In the room there is much-used equipment, a bricked-up chimney, and, of course, a sink with two faucets, imperial windows which open vertically and new carpeting which is clearly concealing the not so good condition of the floor, on the wall there are some primitivist-style reproductions. When my neighbour turns on the faucet, I have the feeling that water is pouring onto my floor. Everything possible is self-service, which causes some problems at the beginning (at breakfast, I am unsure where the bread is, then I have a hard time cutting it, and the toaster is archaic). But it is cosy here, clean, and it doesn't smell of dust. As if I was visiting some distant aunt, but without the need to talk to anyone.

At the beginning I relate to London, too, as the acme of elegance, culture, and peaceful beauty. In the evening I come out of the Museum and go the same way, or more often via Goodge St. to Saville St.

14 February 1999

I'm leaving. Train to the airport is going somewhere still farther. Next to me sits a young girl who's constantly gabbing on the telephone, she has a rather extravagant hairstyle (like an ancient Egyptian) and sandals on her bare legs! The sandals are, in fact, on a thick sole and her toenails are painted, but all the same. Perhaps here people have high blood pressure or some other illnesses which provoke this phenomenon, or they're trying not to surrender to the dictatorship of the seasons. But all the same: sandals on bare feet in February!

I go on. From under the shell of the city a landscape is beginning to peer out: hills in the distance, closer in, segregated by low fences, squares of pastures upon which in groups or scattered stand woolly sheep, by the dump - boggy meadows and plenty of garbage everywhere.

Ventnor, 15.IV.1914 (Wednesday)

Yesterday: morn[ing] work at home, walk to the park, fatigue, quite human, I'm feeling rather sleepy, the pelicans are departing. Work a bit, for about an hour, read *Candida*. Perhaps Shaw's best work; he came upon an essentially dramatic situation and sketched it out well. A singular seaside depression has overtaken me; I know this well from the islands. The sea breathes an emptiness filled with promises; its inviolability lures and then disappoints. Good weather in the afternoon, peace and the everlasting drama of the setting sun. Go towards Shanklin with M[other], with wh[om] rel[ations] have improved a bit. Go on by myself on the landslip. I'm taken by the woods oversaturated with the greenness of moss and ivy; birds sing, the sea whispers very quietly. Among the entangled branches a dark green peers out. I stand on a large mossy rock and experience a metaphysical dissolution into the surroundings; drink passionately, peace, directness, freshness, and reality. Yes, reality. Inspiration evokes a strong need to confirm the reality we have before our selves. Blending in with it. Again the concept of nirvana as a merciless objectivism, as a killing of oneself by a spiritual blending in with nature. The only form of rational suicide. Esoteric meaning of Buddhist philosophy.

Exeter, 21 February 2000

Only after a few days of teaching the international students here (they can't understand why they should feel morally responsible for the evil which their ancestors committed in the name of national values although they feel that national belonging is key for them), I take off to see the cathedral. In contrast to Americans, I can't stand visiting museums or monuments. But the cathedral is wonderful, the further I go in, the more it is wondrous. The naked, high vaulting; I flow into the interior, am floating above the stone floor, drift towards the side naves, towards the next bishops and next princes lying in the whiteness of alabaster or the multicolouredness of marble, towards the next chapels, the next stained-glass windows in these chapels, the next paintings. Beautiful. Embroidered pillows on the seats, on the stone benches running along the walls, on the wooden seats of the central nave. Who embroidered all this? For how many years? An old woman's old hand strokes the wooden plinth at the entrance to the central nave. She smiles as if she were conversing with the wood. As if she had made this gesture already as a young girl, walking through the cathedral and thoughtlessly touching the stone, alabaster, marble, and finally coming across something warm, her hand stays on something smooth, polished by hundreds of hands of English children, retaining their warmth. Her hand hangs at eye level, her mouth smiles nostalgically.

But before I even came in, when I was just approaching the cathedral, but it was already in sight, surrounded by grass, a procession of yellow-navy children slipped by; when they reached the corner of the building, however, a strong wind nearly knocked them over. Suddenly I noticed elegant ladies in hats going out through the main doors: green, blue-red, black. A wedding? I hurry but no bridal couple is to be seen, but from the church, from the main and side doors, a crowd of older women starts to pour out, in hats and without, dressed more or less sophisticatedly, and each is holding a large folder in her hand, grey hair blowing in the wind; they stand disoriented by these drafts, still excited, they converse, go to their cars, or head in the direction of the square, a procession of grey-haired heads, scarves fly, coats flap and open in the wind. Hundreds of old English women exit Exeter Cathedral. 'The 80th Anniversary of the Devon Women's Institutes.'

I return here in the evening; it will start getting good and dark soon but here in the cosy light of lamps, the distinct and pithy tones of the organ. A service is being held, everyone including the choir is in the central nave, the choir sings so beautifully that no one dares to disturb with their amateur version.

[Ventnor] 16.4.1914

Yesterday: Worked in the morning; afternoon, about 3, a boat to Blackgang. The rocking discomfits me a bit, wind on the way back. In my state of physical not-quite-well-being, I don't share a strong exultation in new and strange experiences. The coastline from Ventnor to St Catherine's is gorgeous. An evenly cut wall behind, a table, looking towards the sea is a sheer cliff made of layered chips. At the foot of that cliff begins an easy incline going down towards the sea where the descending terrace is covered with some wondrous greenery. Closer to Ventnor, this incline is cut off by the sea and the coast rises directly from the sea with a white wall of chalk. Farther towards St Cather[ine's] there are gorgeous, emerald meadows which descend easily all the way to the sea itself. I recall an afternoon when N and I travelled around the island; looking at our home in Steephill Cove. My eyes take in the green meadows and trees, still barren, but with rich and lush clumps of a soft and pleasant contour scattered about the meadow. Remember how this landscape once enraptured me and feel once more that I love it. Looking at the paths which I took here then. From beyond St Catherine's (a village which I had not noticed then, it would be good to live there). The sandstone ridge walls, yellow, contrasting strongly with the blue-green sea. The foggy coast of the mainland.

The whole time I dream of such pleasures as I will certainly have in the summer in Australia. I still seem to have some sort of incapability of taking life in directly, especially what it gives me. I must capture each experience as a part of the larger whole, as a detail in a system of something. I think about how wonderful it would be to become a millionaire and own such a Stram launch for oneself. In the evening I work at home and write a *petit poeme en prose* which I composed during the walk to the Cove. I was thinking intensely and a lot about N as well. Hard but with longing, think about T but I try to control myself and clearly be aware of the framework which must be maintained. The end.

Excursion to Paignton, 24 February 2000

The carriages are covered with such a layer of mud that I wonder if I will be able to see anything from inside. But something is visible. For instance, towns of empty camping trailers, identical, identically dead. A small bay at low tide with hopelessly tilted boats stuck in a sticky mud like abandoned lovers. The red cliff covered with a green drapery of vegetation looks like a decoration for some surrealistic play. A small settlement on a bright bank, on the left side the sea, real, and at the very end ships falling off beyond the horizon. A row of houses diminishing and tapering off to absurdity and constantly that idiotic redness of the soil. The sea has become a bay, the water wrinkled, some sea birds sit on the edge. This is Devon. Palms at last (not large), lots of houses: typically English, touching one another, a few distinguished white villas in large gardens, some apartment buildings, some picturesque brick timber wall. Some little red and grey roof tiles, covered with yellow moss or something of the sort. Little ponds with sleepy ducks. Finally Paignton. The train comes into the centre of the city. Cold, windy. I risk a coffee at the coffee-house. Inside a few old women gaping at the void before them, sitting alone at tables and smoking cigarettes. Bright sun. Pathetic espresso. Then I look for the sea, follow the promenade, reach the beach, the red sand, a few beautiful shells, pick some for my children. Retirees with dogs, a small boy gets his shoes wet after a bit of playing near the edge. I feel some sublime mood, the sea in my peasant soul always evokes an epiphany of the absolute.

[Ventnor] 18.4.1914

Today is my last day in Ventnor. Quickly finish reading the Polish [manuscript]. I am already generally taken up by the fervour of the journey. From this point of view, I am v[ery] glad that the matter with T is over. I really will have to concentrate on preparations and try to get everything in order and be efficient. Today I am generally a bit tired (heart) though I'm managing; my work is absorbing me and I drown my sorrows in it. On Thursday I went for a walk towards Shanklin. A beautiful valley in Luccombe Chine. I see before me the entrance to a valley, closed to the public, and socialist reflections come to me. The view from the mountain at Shanklin, the subtly carved out bay, closed off with a white wall and deeper into the island, very pretty. Enthusiasm for the sea; divine elegance, the wondrous and the catastrophic nature of the appearance of the sea. White foam, the symbol of beauty.

Saturday morning, departure from Exeter

Bright morning sun, frozen blades of grass, long shadows of trees. The railway station, clean and the aroma of good coffee, some guy is looking at me, his wife approaches him, in a white hat, fiftyish like him. People sitting on the platform are reflected in the windows of trains, can be confused with those sitting inside them. The conductor closes the yellow doors. Departure. The next train. I get in. A place by the window. A row of Victorian red brick homes, picturesquely untended, blue doors in an arched bay window. Rural residence, a huge home, two-storey with a high roof, next to it various farm buildings and meadows, meadows, meadows. Grey-black sheep which look like motionless heaps of tufts. Just as motionless is a herd of deer, a hare is suspended in mid-leap, birds move their wings helplessly and stand in place. Only the bushes growing on the dump are moving, or maybe it is only one bush which is unfolding its brownish-green substance, glistening in the sun. Water, huge puddles, brownish, churning river. Another flood.

The delusion of the 'reality' of a diary. Diaries are just as unrealistic as other forms of literature or perhaps unreal in some different way. The events about which the diary speaks did really happen, but many other things happened about which the diary says nothing. Diaries are usually written in depression when a person feels a distance from life, from the world, from the self. When one is lost in misanthropy or, quite the opposite, in numerous but superficial contacts. When a person does not even make the effort to find an interlocutor. That is when one finds what is essential in oneself and in contact with nature, observing it, poetry, taking photographs, writing. That is when one looks out the window, twisting the edge of a silk shawl in one's fingers. Observes the sky crossed out by vapour trails, the railway stations of little towns flooded with sun, some indeterminate factories, bleached meadows ...

20.4.1914

London does not serve me well. It's almost impossible to remain in the kind of focus I had yesterday at the seaside. Yesterday I ran to Mrs Dunn for no reason. In the evening at the Borenius's; a piece from the book and an interview with Mrs D steer me into a completely undesirable mood. I think about 'injecting' arsenic. Undifferentiated sens[ibility]. Undoubt[edly] I am defending myself consciously and effectively but it's v[ery] far to the ideal training. Sleeping v[ery] poorly - and thousands of the worst thoughts come to me.

28 February 2000

A nice day, cool. Couldn't get up in the morning, delay the moment of rising, decide to take a shower later. Finally I irrevocably must go downstairs because the Salvation Army won't give me breakfast. Lots of Americans in the dining room, talking about themselves, excited about what they saw the previous day and what they will see today. 'I love museums'. 'The time zones start in London!' 'Have you seen the Millennium Dome?' I wait impatiently for a boiled egg. It's getting more empty. I observe the black waitresses, one of them is humming a song; their world seems hermetically sealed. An older American, horribly wrinkled, chats with the waitress, asks her if she is pregnant for the first time (I hadn't noticed that at all);

the waitress replies with some hesitation as if she was wondering whether she should tell the truth. 'No, second, then?', 'How old is the first one?' (Again after a pause:) 'Twelve!' The American congratulates her, the other woman is laughing, excited by this interest in her. My daughter is also 12 years old.

During the remodelling of the LSE library, the archives have been moved to another building. 25 Southampton Buildings, next to Lincoln's Inn, a section of old London surrounded by a high wall. I take many pictures. A woman in a judge's wig, a Rolls Royce in the parking lot, an imperial lawn, the first crocuses, a red royal mailbox, some dandy chap throwing letters into it. Then I have to only cross Chancery Lane and there it is: between a dully gleaming, dusty skyscraper and a Victorian courtyard with a damp lawn, mossy stone steps and an iron balustrade to which bicycles may not be fastened - in this chilly cul-de-sac is the entrance to the library. And again it is like last year: the excited and hurrying youth, multilingual and multicoloured. After half an hour of filling out forms, I receive my card and go looking for the archives. The maze of corridors is well marked, brass handles say 'Push' and 'Pull', thickly laid paint on the windows, the smell of dust. They bring me boxes with the diaries. I arrange my things comfortably. I try to comprehend the intricacies of M's affairs of the heart, Zakopane 1912. I work hard at deciphering his nervous handwriting, exhale with his Polish, while all around me is the English life of the archives employees.

Lunch with Terry, we discuss the exhibition of M and W photographs, then go together to the RAI on Fitzroy Street. There is no number 16, in its place stands some horrid dormitory for Asian students or something of the sort.

22.4.1914 Wednesday morning

In the afternoon via the Brit[ish] Mus[eum] where I cannot focus my thoughts, to Miss Jones (…) I return on foot through Primrose Hill. There it's always as if I had thrown off my chains. At the time, on the last Saturday of January when she broke it off with me for the second time, I walked there alone in the night, overflowing with energy and joy, with a feeling of freedom and creativity, absolutely decided that I would never return. Yesterday Pri[mrose] Hill was wondrous in a golden halo of green buds which flame with silver and gold against the black trunks of the trees, like the triumph of life over the force of metropolitan mummification. This effect immediately reminds me of T and fills me with sorrow. I recall spring of last year when I was walking through the squares to N towards 16 Fitzroy St and felt the spring mood of an awakening love. How differently I saw her then! Physically and morally. I can remember her face as it looked then perfectly. Yesterday on Prim[rose] Hill an inflow of energy. 'Have to create something new in life, extract the plus ultra. I don't want to move about in a monotonous closed circle of the same tumbles and falls.' I had a moment of decline - I wanted to approach some woman - but I controlled myself. These horrid, dirty instincts - strange how I see her psychology in their light, disgust overtakes me - and those instincts fall away from me automat[ically]. But I alone don't have enough strength to fight them straight on. Repugnant.

29 February 2000

In the afternoon an American comes in, absorbing all the archivists. He is looking for M's things and some other effects as well. He gets them, looks them over. Towards the end of the day he accidentally looks into my box. I must be a Pole because I'm reading the diaries in the original. He is an anthropologist. Publication of the diaries was a shock, but when he went on his own field research, it turned out that it was all true, that that is exactly the way it is. He is pleased that I am involved in this, it is a real service, he also likes my theory that publication of the diaries prompted postmodernism in anthropology. We say goodbye, I pack my computer into my backpack. Walking down the corridors and thinking why do I like this building so much? I could spend the rest of my life here, discovering more and more corridors, some rarely used rooms like the one with the card catalogue: a high ceiling, and, under it, two mercury (?) lamps which light up very slowly, rows of cabinets with drawers, but not so high as in the Jagiellonian Library. I was there twice looking for Andrzej Waligórski's doctoral dissertation from the 1930s. The sound of my own footsteps, some disquiet in the thinned air. Once I ventured through some grey, double doors, went a bit further down a corridor and discovered, under a window looking out on an interior courtyard, a slightly dusty and long unpainted, fantastic radiator: the ribs were cast in an artistic design from which the paint - in a stately shade of ivory - had fallen off. The light, dispersed by the dust on the window, lit up this luxurious item, the sculpting took on more plasticity and the black, wooden knob gleamed with a matt shine. I discover more and more staircases with steps fitted with worn-edged metal, with precisely cast balustrades, and then carefully and repeatedly painted with oil paint, and, parallel to the floor, being part of its homologous outline, a wooden railing which, descending to the ground floor, was capped with a round disc polished by the touch of the hundreds of hands of figures which had run down these stairs. The shadow of semicircular windows falls on a second storey wall, or rather a semicircular light, hatched by the chessboard framing, hangs on the wall of the second story. Sometimes all one hears is the dead bang of a door closing behind someone, deadened by other doors, corridors, and stairs.

Witkiewicz? Why can we still read him? One of the reasons is certainly the fact that W writes with an irony aimed at the world and at himself. Lack of a distancing is a sin which is unforgivable today. After all, distance is a necessary condition for any creativity: geographical distance aids perfectly in writing, that is why anthropology has so much in common with literature. Sometimes it is good to just go somewhere else in order to become a writer (though usually that in itself does not suffice). But after all, it is not really about a geographical distance, but a cultural one. This doesn't mean that one undermines some accepted values in the name of some others. Distance depends upon an ironic suspension of shared norms, or rather on slipping out of the interior of a system onto its peripheries and going back again. Irony is not abnegation. One must believe and simultaneously not believe in something. One has to talk and simultaneously laugh at what one is saying. One has to describe something in enchantment while simultaneously making fun of oneself. One has to nod yes to the fools, and make faces behind their backs. Or even worse: one has to pretend before the fools that those faces are our authentic facial expression (when we know ourselves that we don't have any 'authentic facial expression'). That is exactly how Witkiewicz was, that is why we can read him without aesthetic masochism. That is how M was, too, as the author of Argonauts of the Western Pacific *or* Coral Gardens. *But M from the diaries is not ironic, or at least not autoironic. He wanted to change himself, so he had to treat himself seriously. He treated his natives and himself ironically in monographs and that is why these books are still alive.*

Meet with Helena at lunchtime and walk in Lincoln's Inn Fields, her determined, slightly stooped figure, the community of close relationships with M, wholeheartedness, understanding despite the differences (age, language, heritage), but perhaps some deeper understanding, reaching down into the 'essential' things.

Friday 24.4.1914 [written] in Berlin

Great rush at home; feelings of loneliness: my M[other] and I in the whole wide world. Sadness that I'm leaving M[other]. Departure from Holborn Viaduct.

I am immeas[urably] sad and abandoned. On the train I rec[all] immeas[urably] strongly the ride to Conr[ad's]. Look out through the window at the Thames. This is the way we came back, one memor[y] after another arises of that day and night in Sandgate. This railway line is absol[utely] connected with her. I close my eyes; she comes towards me out of the darkness; I see her more and more clearly as she walks towards me with reproach on her face and stands before me; a vision born of pain and longing; I physically feel her presence. In my ears I hear constantly the motif of hopeless pain from *Parsival*. For the first time since breaking up my thoughts don't leave her for a moment; mad grief that it happened this way. Tearful grief. I don't even have any certainty that I won't go back. I have the feeling that she is going through something similar. At the same time I think to myself that I am tired, weakened, and cannot decide about my internal state. I am not certain what I would do if I had met her just then. Ashford, the station. I rec[all] - with hopel[ess] despair, that chilly morning, 3 persons, she with a newspaper. Her face - a little sparrow - in that hat with the feather. Conrad's voice in French. Then the road. In Folk[estone] I look at the pier, there where we walked together. The ship departs; the double flash of the lighthouse. My eyes wander to the left, there where we walked. This is starting hopelessly, a dull emptiness; the chasm under it all, overflowing with resignation. For all this time, even up to this moment, I have been feeling awfully bad. Pain penetrating everything; 'a feeling that everything has ended' and has been exhausted totally. A pain not human, not individual. One is a piece of suffering matter. Suffering is evenly distributed over the whole body; 'homogenous block of soft, sticky, suffering matter'.

London, 2 March 2000

Once again I tramp along my daily route, this time I stop for coffee, sit at a table on my favourite Lambs Conduit Street. Next to a restaurant with wooden benches on the outside and a golden lamb on the matt-glass window. The dry cleaners, a young Indian man sits in the display window and sews something on a machine. The enigmatic, light blue Biofarm beauty care, the black-gold funeral home in whose clean window is reflected the Delicatessen outside, which is where I'm sitting in the fresh air and sun, drinking a wonderful machiato. Further on is a small bookshop where I once bought Charlotte Bronte's Jane Eyre. *They need someone there for 3 to 5 days a week. Wonder if I could earn enough money there to rent a 2-bedroom flat over Furniture Experience. This piece of the street is closed to everyday traffic, it's cosy. Further down is Simmons Gallery, Vats Wine Bar, the Dental Surgery, Jewellery shop (closed). A young couple with bags in the shape of tennis rackets pass by with a light, springy step. Someone* has gone into the funeral shop, furtively, I didn't even notice who. Three girls, the tallest, long blonde hair, carries a guitar and shouts at the young man who tousles the smallest's hair as he passes them. A crumpled newspaper, pushed by the wind, glides along the pavement behind the pedestrians like a dog. And then there's Red Lion Street with numerous restaurants but without the charm of Lambs Conduit.

M and I were both fascinated with England, but in the case of M it was a prima factum fascination, and in mine something of a sort of déja vu. In England I feel unexpectedly good, as if I had found myself in my natural environment. I like English cities with their nonchalance and English landscape with its clear air, I like the English because they don't bother me, and I love a few English women, like Shirley and Helena, because they are as close to me as my Lutheran aunts, or Krystyna who is like the sister I don't have. English women-students loved M because he treated them seriously. And concurrently he was an element of the anti-world, like them. Like me. Anthropology is born of such ambivalence. And so is art.

I feel pangs of conscience about M. He wrote only for himself. But not me - therein lies the difference. Though, as others would have it, in going to the

English cities with their nonchalance

Shirley ... as close to me as my lutheran aunts

trouble of writing, we always count on some reader, even if that person is no other than ourselves. How would something that I would write only to myself look? There would be more of me, my inside self. Yet I am, after all, in this here as well: reflected in the glass of the display windows and, as a friend of mine has put it, one sees my scars in what I write. Yes.

Translated by Annamaria Orla-Bukowska
Photos by Grazyna Kubica

Five Poems

First writing of the New Year

The lawn is steeped in green,
vivid under dissolving snow.

Above my desk, a fleck of jade
has appeared on the cornice -

one inexplicable lacewing.

If I remain still, in time
the light will modulate

visibly. Only by leaving
can the goldfinch in the camellia

ignite that flare of brilliance,
that pang of poignancy.

1st January 2001
Gregory Warren Wilson

Col Agnel

Climbing from one belvedere to the next
through high birdsong, the last of the cows
behind, their bells receding, streams
reversed to an icy dribble;

cairn succeeded by cross
on a widening skyline, ridges stretched
over a mattress of cloud, the distant iced cones
of Mont Blanc, Monte Rosa;

and on and up to the flattened U
of the pass, rare grass, the stone marking
the border. Standing in turn
one foot in la France, the other in l'Italia:

the families, old couples who've driven up
from both sides, braving the ride
of vertiginous hairpin bends
to stare into one another's countries

to find they are looking into a mirror
at their own valleys, mountains
layered in blue, people
shading their eyes and gesturing

just as they do, their excited breath
fused in the air on a day without mist
or grey, a day so extraordinary clear
nothing needs translating.

Caroline Price

The boy inheritor of the earth and his picture machine

I look at butterflies all day
Skippers and Tiger Swallowtails,
Cleopatras, Adonis Blues and Blue
Morpho: the Madagascan Sunset
moth. All still. Un-flying.
Butter creatures.

And I prepare myself, every time,
in case they ask my name:
Hero.
The Giant.
The King. That is me.

>   Look. I have another roll,
>   This one is the entire zoo. See?
>   What more do you want?
>   What more?

Hisham Matar

Wings

I waited for my father
to come home from work
sitting on the doorstep
rolling my marble
with the bright orange wings inside
at the smaller ones
lined up along the kerb.
I gave myself points
for every hit.
Practised the tricky, flicking movement
with finger and thumb.
You can't play marbles
the Italian boy from next door scoffed
I ignored him.
I wanted to be alone
to think about the fight I'd had
with Linda Coleman
on the railway bridge
after school that day,
the second fight
we'd had that week,
how all the girls had lined up shouting
and how Jacqueline Bromley
had stuck up for me.
I wanted to plan what I
might do next time
the way I sometimes lay awake
in bed with my thoughts
though my sisters were there
arguing and pushing for space.
I almost lost my prize marble down the drain
when my father turned the corner
and I looked up.

Frances Angela

Diagnostic

How well pain
Educates her body
To its subtle plan

Tissue and bone
Knitted round the Cactus
Growing in her spine

Prostrate she waits
For Lady Sciatica
To start the dance

Left leg wired
To the shock machine
Her hands beat time

Cocooned in illness
Beyond the reach
Of pills, her plaints

Grow monstrous, thick
With triumphs scored
Against the young

Now in my turn
Upon the rack
I learn the arts

Of self deception
Scrupulously, at last
My mother's son

Phil Cohen

A barbarous history

Nicholas Waddell

Ludo De Witte, *The Assassination of Lumumba*, Verso, £17
Michela Wrong, *In the Footsteps of Mr Kurtz*, Fourth Estate, £7.99

When asked about their namesake, a blank look was all I got from the man at
'Lumumba Autospares' in the Tanzanian capital Dar es Salaam. The headmaster
of 'Lumumba Primary School' told me that Lumumba was the first leader of
independent Congo but he thought that it was a plane crash that killed him.[1]
Such comments are painfully ironic given that the last letter that Lumumba
ever wrote contained the following words:

> History will one day have its say; it will not be the history taught in the
> United Nations, Washington, Paris, or Brussels, however, but the history
> taught in the countries that have rid themselves of colonialism and its
> puppets. Africa will write its own history, and both north and south of the
> Sahara it will be a history full of glory and dignity.

The famous scene with which the Belgian writer and sociologist Ludo De Witte
opens *The Assassination of Patrice Lumumba* encapsulates both what Lumumba
represented and what he fought against. It is June 1960 in the Congolese capital,
Léopoldville (now Kinshasa). Sovereignty is being handed over from Belgium
to the newly elected representatives of the Congolese people. 'The
independence of Congo', announces King Baudouin of Belgium, 'is the result
of the undertaking conceived by the genius of King Léopold II'. 'Don't replace

---

1. For the sake of simplicity, I have referred to 'Congo' throughout this piece. In 1971,
   Congo was renamed Zaire by Mobutu. When Kabila took power in 1997 the country
   became the Democratic Republic of Congo.

the structures that Belgium hands over to you', the Congolese are instructed, 'until you are sure you can do better'. Despite independence, 'we will remain by your side'. To the total astonishment of the Belgians, Lumumba takes the floor in an unscheduled address that shatters the paternalistic charade in progress. Lumumba speaks of an independence won from below rather than bestowed from above. He speaks over the assembled Belgian notables and addresses 'Congolese men and women, fighters for independence, who are today victorious'. Across the nation hushed crowds are gathered around radios, craning their necks to catch every word of a language that many Congolese thought could not be spoken to Europeans. There is a moment of incredible release. Lumumba has not only issued a slap to the face of colonialism, he has also offended the nascent neo-colonial order.

In his preface to *Animal Farm*, Orwell described how, in free societies, 'Unpopular ideas can be silenced, and inconvenient facts kept dark, without any need for an official ban'. Thus it has taken forty years for the definitive account of one of the most important political assassinations of the twentieth century - that of Patrice Lumumba - to appear. Until now, the prevailing story of the murder of the first Prime Minister of independent Congo has been that it was, as one Belgian general put it, a 'Bantu affair': Lumumba was a casualty of the brutal nature of African politics and any Belgian involvement was limited to a handful of junior officials acting under Congolese command. Penetrating the intricate web of falsification that has sustained it, De Witte shoots this tale to pieces. Accusations of Western involvement in Lumumba's death are by no means new, but the rigour with which De Witte makes his case is. In a staggering indictment of the ruthlessness and moral bankruptcy of Western governments and the institutions they control, he amasses a huge body of evidence implicating the USA, the UN and Belgium. The resulting volume, which took seven years to research, prickles with fury and political commitment. In Belgium the uproar provoked by the book was such that the Belgian parliament was pressured into establishing a commission of inquiry into Belgium's part in Lumumba's death.

It is not difficult to see why Sartre described Lumumba as 'a meteor in the African firmament'. Completely unknown to the Congolese people in 1955, by 1958 Lumumba was a nationalist beacon. In 1960 he was elected Prime Minister; it was a position he would hold for only ten weeks. Rather than risk being swept along in the dramatically swift radicalisation of Congolese politics, in 1960 Belgium abruptly decided to grant its colony independence. Things, however, did not go as smoothly as planned. As De Witte sums up with characteristic force:

> Almost a hundred years earlier, Léopold II had had a marble medallion carved with the saying: 'Belgium needs a colony'. This dream had come true. But to preserve the benefits of colonialism for the future, they needed to establish in Léopoldville a regime with which they could do business. Patrice Lumumba was standing in the way.

Nowhere was 'business' more relevant than in the Congolese province of Katanga. Dripping in mineral wealth, Katanga was effectively owned and run by Belgian mining houses and the Belgian ruling classes intended it to remain that way. When it became clear that Belgian interests stood to be compromised, Belgium engineered Katanga's secession. (One Belgian minister described the Katangan president, Moïse Tshombe, as 'necessary to provide a veneer of legality … a good cover to have'.) As De Witte writes, Belgium's actions effectively 'amputated Katanga from the body of the Congo in the hope that Léopoldville would not survive the operation'.

Survival was no easy task for the newly independent state. In an attempt to quash the secession and restore territorial integrity to Congo, President Kasa Vubu and Prime Minister Lumumba appealed to the UN to intervene. In practice, and as De Witte powerfully conveys, UN intervention served to consolidate secession as the UN colluded with Western intentions to sabotage Lumumba's administration. Feeling betrayed by the UN and facing attempts by Western media to discredit him, Lumumba sought the support of African allies and the USSR. Again, he was blocked by the UN.

Not content with merely manipulating Congolese politics and cultivating international opposition to Lumumba, Belgium and the US considered more drastic action. President Eisenhower was warned by his CIA chief that 'Lumumba … remained a grave danger as long as he was not disposed of'. Hit men were approached, and a plan to poison Lumumba was drawn up. Similarly, the Belgian Minister of African Affairs called for Lumumba's *'élimination définitive'*. Telegram traffic was heavy with messages to the same effect. Belgium's defenders have argued that such words imply nothing more than Lumumba's *political* immobilisation. De Witte leaves the credibility of such a position in tatters.

Lumumba did not have long to wait. Following a power struggle with President Kasa Vubu, American-backed Joseph Mobutu seized power. Lumumba was placed under house arrest for his 'protection'. He escaped but was recaptured by Mobutu's soldiers, along with two supporters, after the UN withheld its protection. Still, Lumumba remained an intolerable liability for his enemies. The danger that he might yet reap the harvest of his popular support was ever present. It was this risk that sealed his fate.

De Witte comes into his own in chronicling Belgium's role in Lumumba's bloody end. He establishes beyond doubt that the Prime Minister's Belgian-backed transfer to Katanga amounted to a death sentence. On the way to the Katangan principal city of Elisabethville, Lumumba was brutally beaten by Mobutu's soldiers and force-fed tufts of hair that had been torn from his head. Earlier, soldiers had tried to humiliate him by stuffing into his mouth the statement in which he had described himself as the head of the country's democratically elected government. Further beatings followed.

Previously, in accounts such as that of Jacques Brassine, such horrors have been blamed on the Congolese. De Witte, however, provides clear evidence of Belgian participation. On 17 January 1961 a convoy of cars carrying Belgian soldiers and Katangan ministers drove the three prisoners into a forest and shot them. A few nights later, in an effort to destroy the evidence, a small party headed by two Belgians exhumed the bodies of Lumumba and his allies. With considerable difficulty, hacksaws were used to cut them up. The pieces were then thrown into a barrel of sulphuric acid. What could not be dissolved was ground up and scattered. One of the Belgian police commissioners who carried out the operation would later show journalists two of Patrice Lumumba's teeth that he had kept as souvenirs. Intricate lies about his murder were spun as Belgium proclaimed its total innocence and Lumumba was vilified by Western commentators.

As De Witte makes clear, the significance of Lumumba's murder goes beyond the particulars of the case. Systemic features of the relationship between the West and the so-called 'less developed' countries are distilled in the details of the actions of Belgium, the USA and the UN. De Witte contends that Soviet overtures to Lumumba were not the prime reason why Lumumba encountered the wrath of the West. He argues that, rather than a matter of Cold War expediency, Lumumba's death was a result of the Western perception that 'Congolese independence was primarily an expression of the anti-colonial revolution which pitted the colonialist North against the colonised South.' De Witte continues:

> Just as the Belgian King, Léopold II, had legitimised the conquest of the
> Congo by presenting it as liberating Africans from the hands of Arab slave
> traders, and colonial exploitation had been justified as a civilising enterprise,
> so in 1960 the nationalists were destroyed in the name of protecting Africa
> from Soviet imperialism.

It was Lumumba's efforts to slip the economic leash of neo-colonialism that set alarm bells ringing. His internationalist beliefs also raised fears about the position of the West in central Africa overall. The independent Congolese Prime Minister had embarked on a course that was unacceptable to Western interests and the only way to reset that course permanently, Western interests decided, was to have him killed.

Although the US and Britain hardly emerge well from the book, Belgium and the UN earn De Witte's most scathing criticism. 'It was', he writes, 'Belgian advice, Belgian orders and finally Belgian hands that killed Lumumba on the 17 January 1961'. Belgium's sins are not only in the past. As De Witte commented at the book's launch, 'the pillars of the Belgian establishment that are implicated in Lumumba's assassination are still in place today'. As for the UN, De Witte repeats the question of a man whose disillusionment with the organisation was total: 'How', asked Lumumba, 'does a blue armband [of the UN] vaccinate against the racism and paternalism of people whose only vision of Africa is lion hunting, slave markets and colonial conquest; people for whom the history of civilisation is built on the possession of colonies?' Ghana's pan-Africanist leader Kwame Nkrumah described Lumumba's assassination as 'the first time in history that the legal ruler of a country has been done to death with the open connivance of a world organisation in whom that ruler put his trust'.

The book never pretends to be a dispassionate evaluation of Lumumba's strengths and weaknesses, or of the brand of nationalism he espoused. As a largely uncritical portrayal of Lumumba, it leaves little space for consideration of flawed political strategies or personal limitations. De Witte suggests that Lumumba might have achieved great things had he lived, but his belief that this might have included creating the conditions for a revolution by the Congolese masses needs more support than De Witte provides. Detailed and factually dense, *The Assassination of Lumumba* does not make light reading. De Witte has stated that he was not concerned to produce a 'faction-thriller'. Instead, '*The Assassination of Lumumba* can be read as the public prosecutor's closing address in the courtroom'. As such, it is supremely effective.

De Witte has not only written of the dramatic death of one man. He has also illuminated the wider political and economic forces that are integral to understanding that death and to the subsequent course of Congolese history. Ultimately, the book's achievement lies not so much in the conclusions it reaches; Raoul Peck's award winning film *Lumumba* (2001) for example, tells a similar tale of the West's role in Lumumba's death. Rather, it is the scholarly rigour with which De Witte has made his case that makes the book so important, and so difficult for his detractors to dismiss.

Though Michela Wrong picks up the story of the man who seized power at Lumumba's expense, *In the Footsteps of Mr Kurtz* is a very different species of book. Thanks in part to Conrad's masterpiece *The Heart of Darkness*, few countries in Africa hold the place that Congo does in the Western imagination. Riding on this fact, Wrong explains that her book draws on the side of Conrad's work that is an 'attack on the history of contemporary colonial behaviour' - an attack that often gets buried amid the clichés the book has spawned about a dark, savage continent. In contrast to De Witte's close focus on specific events and detailed primary research, Michela Wrong is distinguished by her efforts to wring grim humour out of Congo's tragic disintegration. Framed around Wrong's experiences in Congo as a journalist for Reuters, the BBC and the *Financial Times* at the time of Mobutu's downfall, *In The Footsteps of Mr Kurtz* loosely charts the dictator's rise, reign, and fall. Along the way, Wrong considers what (and, more fittingly, who) enabled his rotten regime to survive for so long.

'Why hire a lawyer when you can buy a judge?' was the joke about Kenya's legal system. For most of the 32 years in which he ruled it, however, Mobutu's Congo was the HQ of corruption in Africa. 'Big Man rule', writes Wrong, 'had been encapsulated in one timeless brand: leopardskin toque, Buddy Holly glasses and the carved cane'. The dinosaur who fancied himself as a leopard was widely viewed as representative of all that was wrong with African leadership. His spectacular ousting in 1997 and the collapse, with him, of the ultimate kleptocracy was heralded in *Soundings* as being, 'apart from the end of apartheid, the most symbolic and heartening event on the African continent for the three decades since colonial rule cracked and began to dissolve'.[2]

Yet optimism for Congo's future swiftly dissolved as the region was engulfed in a bewilderingly complex war involving the armies of six African countries as well as numerous non-governmental groups. Congo's history is no exception to the rule which suggests that the mineral wealth of African nations is often directly proportional to the suffering that this wealth causes. As Wrong shows, under Mobutu the Congolese people experienced not so much a 'trickle-down' as a bleeding dry. In fact, the fabulous profits from Congo's wealth travelled in every direction but down. As Wrong shows, it was invariably hoovered up and siphoned off into presidential bank accounts held abroad. Such activities were, writes Wrong, 'coyly referred to by the World Bank and International Monetary Fund as "uncompensated sales" or "leakages"'.

Mobutu conducted operations in a style all his own. Yet Wrong demonstrates how he also picked up where King Léopold had left off. Taking her cue from Adam Hochschild's masterful *King Leopold's Ghost*, Wrong shows that the differences between Léopold and the 'leopard' were less dramatic than Belgian history would have us believe. As Wrong writes, 'the seeds of Mobutuism found fertile ground in which to sprout'.

Wrong is in her element when describing how Mobutu disposed of this wealth. She describes a man whose sense of the common good extended only as far as his entourage. Mobutu accumulated innumerable exclusive properties across Europe. Most obscene of all, however, was the presidential citadel dubbed his 'Versailles in the jungle'. 700 miles from the Congolese capital, this enclave boasted musical fountains, ornamental lakes, private zoos, golden pagodas and a palace covering 15,000 square metres filled with Italian marble, French antiques and Venetian glassware. Among incredible

---

2. Victoria Brittain and Rakia Omaar, *Soundings* 7, p98.

items on the Mobutu shopping list that Wrong reveals is an estimated $65,000 bill for a wedding cake that was flown in from Paris for his daughter. One source is quoted as commenting that the president and his clan 'chartered Boeings like most people use supermarket trolleys'.

If awards were to be given for corruption in the twentieth century, Mobutu would win first prize - in the lifetime achiever category. But, and this is a central point in Wrong's book, an honest acceptance speech would offer thanks to his creditors, and mention 'all those without whom it would not have been possible'. This list would be a long one. Special mention would have to go to the World Bank, the IMF, France, Belgium, Swiss bankers, the CIA and US presidents and advisors. Between them the USA and France alone contributed billions of dollars to propping up their Cold War ally. President George Bush counted Mobutu as 'one of our most valued friends'. Mobutu did not operate in a vacuum. It is convenient for numerous parties to play down the fact that many hands fed and oiled the regime that caused the Congolese people and their neighbours so much misery. Wrong remarks how '*Mea culpa*' was a sentiment conspicuous by its absence during her interviews with 'the Washington financiers who granted billions to a known thief, whose institutions will one day have to explain why the Congolese should be held responsible for loans made in bad faith'.

'By the end of the century', writes Wrong, 'the government's annual operating budget for what is potentially one of Africa's richest states was dipping below the daily takings of the US superstore Wal-Mart'. What she describes as Congo's 'Alice in Wonderland finances' saw inflation balloon to 9,800 per cent in 1994 (the price of goods changed before people had time to hand over the bags of notes required to pay for them). Wrong shows how for a long time the rich were able to buy themselves into a parallel universe, insulated from the 'inconveniences' of crumbling infrastructure and economic freefall: 'Road non-existent? Buy a four-wheel drive. National television on the blink? Install a satellite dish in your back garden and tune in to CNN. Phone out of order? Hire a Telecel.' Like a crazy game of building blocks, in which parts of the underlying structure are successively removed to build it higher and higher, Mobutu's regime eventually became so precarious that it required only the lightest push to topple it. This final shove came in the form of the band of Ugandan and Rwandan-backed rebels led by Laurent Kabila. This time there would be no French or any other troops to bail Mobutu out. Not only had the geo-political climate changed. The regional power balance had also shifted, when the Rwandese Patriotic Front wrestled control of Rwanda from the genocidal Hutu extremists. Wrong conveys how the corner into which Mobutu had backed himself was so tight that it was all he could do to escape alive as his army evaporated around him. Having taken refuge in Morocco, Mobutu died in September 1997.

While much of the book is evocative and elegantly told, Wrong's prose is overwritten in places and, at times, offensive. When many racist perceptions of Africa emphasise wildlife over people (often suggesting little distinction between the two), the following description of Congolese street traders is not insignificant. Wrong observes them 'like watching predators on the savannah as they prowled the long grasses and scored the horizon, searching relentlessly for a kill'. Wrong dehumanises a disabled man that she meets, describing him as a 'vision of horror, the kind of logic-defying deformity that rises gibbering and scrabbling from the depths of the subconscious at night'.

In *The Footsteps of Mr Kurtz* takes broad and for the most part well-measured strides across Congolese history, and Michela Wrong serves up a readily digestible blend of political analysis, travel writing and history. But books such as this one tread a fine line between spanning different genres - achieved with haunting brilliance in Philip Gourevitch's writings on Rwanda - and falling between them. There are sections when Wrong's book spreads itself too wide and too thin, the coverage of the Rwandan genocide being a case in point. *In The Footsteps of Mr Kurtz* provides neither a thorough account of Mobutu's reign from the top, nor of what it really meant for the Congolese people. (The latter would be a less entertaining and more sobering, disconcerting tale than the one Wrong has chosen to tell.) The result is a work that lacks a centre of gravity, whose strands do not form an entirely coherent whole.

Nevertheless, Wrong provides a corrective to those who believe it is time to stop harping on about imperialism, that the track record since decolonisation shows that Africans themselves must bear full responsibility for their continent's dire predicament. Wrong has written a compelling narrative whose primary strength lies in its accessibility and the way that it resists pinning all the evils of the Mobutu regime on Mobutu the individual. Wrong's conclusion that Congo's profound problems are rooted in a barbarous colonial history succeeded by ruthless Western behaviour ever since is one that applies across the continent and beyond.

A sense of occasion

Richard Clayton

David Herd, John Ashbery and American Poetry, Manchester University Press

Even now, after a forty-year writing career, Guggenheim and MacArthur Fellowships and numerous awards, John Ashbery still divides critical opinion like no other contemporary poet. His most recent volume *Your Name Here*, published in 2000, exemplifies the trend. For Harold Bloom, self-styled executor of the literary canon, 'Ashbery augments in poetic splendour in his seventies'. *Your Name Here* takes its place alongside the late works of Hardy, Yeats and Wallace Stevens as 'one of the enduring monuments in the language'. But the poet and critic Vernon Scannell finds the effect 'irritatingly camp and silly'. So, which is it?

There is, as might be said of a literature exam paper, no right or wrong answer. To a great extent, it is a matter of taste - but Ashbery has come to represent far more than his own oeuvre. Attitudes to Ashbery are broadly emblematic of attitudes to what poetry should be about, and even what it should try to achieve. As is often the case when people begin jumping on bandwagons, what is actually going on in Ashbery's poems tends to be overlooked. The fact that he is believed to be 'difficult' to read often means he is not 'read' at all'.

For a long time, interviews with Ashbery were virtual inquisitions - the interviewer demanding to know why he wrote so unconventionally. Needless to say, this did not endear Ashbery to the interview process, as this exchange shows:

Interviewer Everyone speaks about the difficulty of your poetry and it seems to me that any discussion of your work must center around what is, or what seems to be, the core of your poem, of your poetry, of your work.

Ashbery I don't know what that core is. Maybe it would help if you explained exactly what you mean by 'difficulty'.

Interviewer The difficulty of language, for one, of syntax. Reading one of your poems, one is not prepared for the kinds of juxtapositions that occur in many of the poems.

Ashbery I don't think one is prepared for juxtapositions in general, is one?'

Although it's never wise to generalise, this perception of Ashbery has resulted from a certain queasiness about what is seen as 'academic' verse. Ashbery's poems are not confessional - they play games with poetic form. At the same time, he includes snippets of 'found' texts, overheard conversations, advertising copy and prose. This has led some critics to accuse him of being dilettante, nonsensical, obscure. In the UK, the battle-lines were traditionally staked out with *The Times Literary Supplement* and *Poetry Review* Ashbery-baiting on one side, and *The London Review of Books* and *Stand* advocating him on the other. There has since been more of an accommodation, with Ashbery now widely recognised, if not fully appreciated, by the British poetry establishment.

Those who do criticise, on both sides of the Atlantic, do so almost out of a sense of grievance. They feel short-changed because Ashbery doesn't provide the requisite 'twist', the single, telling insight. To be sure, there are 'poems about paintings and poems about poems' - which, for poet Michael Donaghy, are 'two terminal symptoms of academic verse' - but everyday life, in its most prosaic and surprising forms, is present in Ashbery's poems to an unprecedented extent.

The achievement of David Herd's book, *John Ashbery and American Poetry*, is to show that not only are there rewarding ways of reading Ashbery, but that his fundamental aim is to draw the reader into a new relationship with the poem. Far from being the random solipsist, Ashbery possesses a 'radically democratic' spirit and an acutely post-modern sensibility.

The tendency to describe Ashbery's poetry as 'academic' is largely due to his adoption by a number of progressive critics in the US, or else an assumption that avant-garde writing is best left to the campus. But when he came down to New York from Harvard in summer 1949, 'academic' was the last word Ashbery would have used to refer to his poetry. The prevailing literary culture, which Herd takes care to evoke, was dominated by the stuffy manners of the New Critics and the stylistic carapace of Robert Lowell's early work. For Ashbery's friend and fellow poet Frank O'Hara, such 'cultivated blandness' was a dead end.

Herd contrasts Lowell's formal, introspective, 'thematic' verse with the more improvised, open and 'occasional' poetic that Ashbery, O'Hara and others were developing. The derivation of 'theme' is from the Greek for deposit, suggesting, as Herd points out, 'that which endures time and resists change'. Lowell's aesthetic - deliberate, monumental, aspiring to transcend its circumstances - had much in common with the stiff rhetoric of post-war American politics. But Ashbery's circle - living and working in the New York of Abstract Expressionism - saw that this sort of language was out-of-step with contemporary reality.

Ashbery's sense of poetic 'occasion' is, according to Herd, an amalgam of his reading of Pasternak, Stevens and William James and his wish - along with O'Hara, Kenneth Koch and James Schuyler - to step around the looming shadow of Lowell. Together, these poets extended the scope of occasional poetry - traditionally, that which is written to mark weddings, births and particular events - to filter a new, impressionistic language.

In 1951, O'Hara was delighted to find the critic Paul Goodman echoing their thoughts in an article on avant-garde writing. 'Occasional poetry', wrote Goodman, is the 'highest kind' because 'it gives the most real and detailed subject-matter, it is closest in its effect on the audience, and it poses the enormous problem of being plausible to the actuality and yet creatively imagining something, finding something unlooked-for'. This amounted to 'marrying the world', as O'Hara put it. Much of Ashbery's poetry is devoted to finding a language appropriate to the moment it is describing ('being plausible to the actuality'), while trying to uncover that 'something unlooked-for' which gives it coherence.

Herd reveals Boris Pasternak as a defining influence in this approach. Ashbery discovered Pasternak as an undergraduate and seems to have been impressed by his theorising. 'People nowadays', Pasternak wrote in 1922, 'imagine that art is like a fountain, whereas it is a sponge. They think art has to flow forth, whereas what it has to do is absorb and become saturated'. Pasternak also evinced a distinctly post-modern idea about artistic production: 'The clearest, most memorable and important feature of art is how it arises ... the finest works ... tell us of their own birth'.

These two strands - the sponginess of his writing and its concern with its own production - are discernible through each phase of Ashbery's career. They lie behind his extraordinary linguistic suppleness and contingent, unanchored representations of self. They offer a reason why he decides to include in his poems those stray thoughts that enter his mind as he writes. As the poet and critic Charles Simic has observed: 'All points of view are temporary to him. He seems to be everywhere and nowhere in his poems'. That is not to say, however, that Ashbery's poetry ultimately signifies nothing. 'It has been axiomatic', says Herd, 'to American writing [since Emerson] that the object of literary understanding is not the text but the world'.

Ashbery attempts to represent the world - in true Pasternakian fashion - by articulating the background, giving prominence to seemingly inconsequential details and putting in more than he leaves out. In doing so, Herd believes, he continues the pragmatist tradition of William James, 'whereby ideas [and, consequently, works of art] are true just in so far as they help us to get into satisfactory relation with other parts of our experience'. This brings Herd to the crux of his argument. Ashbery leads readers to water but he can't make them drink. The meaning of the poems depends on what the reader recognises in Ashbery's snapshots of experience and makes his or her own. Ashbery himself has noted that the 'ideal situation for the poet is to have the reader speak the poem'. Herd explains:

> If the reader were able to speak the poem, the poet would have brought him or her into such a state of understanding, into such a satisfactory relation to the occasion, that the utterance appropriate to that occasion had become apparent to all concerned; as apparent, perhaps, as the next line in the wedding service. Short of this ideal, the keenest pleasure in Ashbery is arriving at the poem within the poem, the poem for which everything else has been a preparation.

Rather than being wilfully abstruse, Ashbery is concerned with communication and, furthermore, with the conditions of communication in 'liberal-democratic culture'. Herd cites Habermas to illustrate how difficult genuine communication is at a time when contemporary society 'calls into question all the "meanings and norms previously fixed by tradition"'. In order to have meaningful dialogue,

Habermas argues, people need to agree on the context of the discussion. Attempting, like Walt Whitman in his time, to forge a new 'solidarity' of understanding, is what Herd regards as Ashbery's 'radically democratic' impulse. As Ashbery himself conceives it:

> Suddenly the street was
> Bananas and the clangor of Japanese instruments.
> Humdrum testaments were scattered around. His head
> Locked into mine. We were a seesaw. Something
> Ought to be written about how this affects
> You when you write poetry:
> The extreme austerity of an almost empty mind
> Colliding with the lush, Rousseau-like foliage of its desire to
> communicate
> Something between breaths, if only for the sake
> Of others and their desire to understand you and desert you
> For other centers of communication, so that understanding
> May begin, and in doing so be undone.

If Ashbery's intentions here are reasonably explicit, elsewhere he is more gnomic. Herd makes sense of Ashbery's most controversial volume, *The Tennis Court Oath,* by suggesting it was a deliberate exercise in obfuscation. Written in Paris in the early 1960s after the moderate reception of his first book, *Some Trees,* these poems enact the problems and difficulties of communication rather than try to resolve them. In our age of political spin and media clamour, it is perhaps easier to see what Ashbery meant by 'the newspaper is ruining your eyes'.

Herd plots the changing phases of Ashbery's writing with skill but his book is not, in any sense, a biography. Although he considers Ashbery's response (in *A Wave*) to the crisis of AIDS, he does not address the poet's sexuality. Herd acknowledges that 'Ashbery's much-stated antagonism to confessional poetry might seem like an epistemology of the closet', but, he believes, Ashbery is 'antipathetic' to this type of poetry 'because it fetishizes the individual ... Ashbery's life enters his writing only in so far as his life, like everybody else's, is shaped by "what is taking place about us"'.

When he became an overnight success - *Self-Portrait in a Convex Mirror* won the treble of Pulitzer Prize, National Book Award and National Book Critics' Circle Award in 1979 - Ashbery, often his own shrewdest critic, remarked that he had passed from 'unacceptability to acceptance without an intervening period of appreciation'. Maybe because of his emergence in the avant-garde coterie of the 'New York School', Ashbery has always been wary of the homogenising grasp of the canon. In his own critical writing, he has made much of 'the other tradition' of lesser-known authors as a source of vitality and invention. Herd suggests that suspicion of being appropriated and limited by the demands of success has been a defining feature of Ashbery's work over the last twenty years.

'Against all the odds', Herd writes, 'Ashbery's poetic has become an orthodoxy. His gestures have become reducible to a shorthand. His style has become a manner. His way of writing has hardened into the kind of reality-denying formulation it evolved to resist.' How does Ashbery respond? By continuing to write at a prolific rate, perhaps with one eye on posterity, by trying to keep up with the pace of events and ceaseless change.

> We sure live in a bizarre and furious
> galaxy, but now it's up to us to make it
> into an environment for maps to sidle up to,
> as trustingly as leeches. Heck, put *us*
> on the map, while you're at it.
> That way we can smoke a cigarette, and stay and sway,
> Shooting the breeze with night and her swift promontories.

Herd might quibble with Harold Bloom's terminology but he clearly believes Ashbery will be and should be read. It is hard to disagree. But the poet *is* anxious about his legacy. In a recent, almost autobiographical poem, 'This Room', Ashbery feels the reader may be absent:

> The room I entered was a dream of this room.
> Surely all those feet on the sofa were mine.
> The oval portrait
> of a dog was me at an early age.

Something shimmers, something is hushed up.

We had macaroni for lunch every day
except Sunday, when a small quail was induced
to be served to us. Why do I tell you these things?
You are not even here.

The market for poetry is small - for Ashbery, often, smaller still. A generous, intelligent guide to Ashbery's work, *John Ashbery and American Poetry* is a consummate manual. By no means prescriptive, it rather inspires the reader to do-it-themselves, to engage with the poetry. As the words *Your Name Here* - published after Herd completed his study - suggest, this is just what Ashbery wants.

Living together, drifting apart

Jo Littler

Yasmin Alibhai-Brown, *Who Do We Think We Are? Imagining the New Britain*, Allen Lane £18.99

A group of Sikh, Muslim, English, Irish, Afro-Caribbean pensioners are ruminating in a park in Southall. They are discussing the erosion of their old ways and the careless young who have foolishly cast off so much of value. They might laugh ruefully. When they don't understand they lean towards each other and try again. They touch the odd elbow in an act of natural intimacy. A Sikh war veteran opens a tiffin and brings out some pakoras. Drinks appear from another bag. The women talk to each other about the rising cost of M&S cardigans. Maybe someone shuffles a pack of cards ... Why does this seem absurd even to imagine?

Comic in its current implausibility, this imaginary scene is used in the introduction to *Who Do We Think We Are?* to dramatise Yasmin Alibhai-Brown's key point that Britain is not the happy land of multicultural integration that some would apparently have us believe. The image of the united pensioners is used to dramatise her argument that 'Britain is getting more tribal and separate', more divided, 'more clannish', a situation which, as she points out, 'does not bode well'. Now all the more prescient in retrospect, *Who Do We Think We Are?* was written before the summer riots took place in culturally segregated and working-class communities in northern de-industrialised towns, during which 'race' became the scapegoat for impoverishment.

Like the rest of the book, and the question which forms its title, the scene with the old people on the bench is also used in another way: to ask why on earth *should* it be absurd to imagine? It functions as a call to activate more work towards change, as well as to point out the lack of it. *Who Do We Think We Are?* therefore addresses a broad audience - the 'we' being anyone in Britain - and aims to address 'how complex and interconnected our lives and needs are now [and] to crack open some of the circumscribed ways we have so far chosen to interpret them'. Whilst arguing for further recognition of the multifaceted ways in which persistent racism shapes Britain's public and private institutions, then, it is also arguing for continual cross-community dialogue about how to achieve change. This makes Alibhai-Brown more in tune with Gramsci's 'pessimism of the intellect, optimism of the will' maxim, rather than being, in her own words, 'some irrelevant, soft-centred liberal who believe[s] in beige coloured piano keys'.

Who Do We Think We Are? contains numerous pithy summaries of a mass of existing literature about ethnicity and Britishness. The subjects of its chapters include the history of immigration and race relations, the structural racism of the media industry, the effects of education practice and policy, and feminism's ignorance of and engagement with issues of ethnicity. To say that this is a book that summarises contemporary and historical debates is not to dispute its 'originality'. It is rather to pay homage, firstly to the often underrated and indispensible genre to which such books belong, and secondly to the skill with which that genre is developed here. Multiple connections between theories, histories and stories of Britishness are seamlessly woven together through Yasmin Alibhai-Brown's provocative writing. This is nicely indicated by the cover, in which the shock-advertising image of a browned-up Queen Elizabeth from the Benetton magazine *Colors*, rather than being used to sell the products of sweated labour, is here articulated to a useful set of debates about ethnicity and 'the establishment'. Such an approach, which winds together salient, vivid detail with an intimate knowledge of academic and political debates, means that this works both as a book for those with a longstanding interest in the subjects of Britishness and the politics of 'race', and as a starter-text introducing readers to new areas.

This was at least the conclusion of the majority of the undergraduate students to whom I gave extracts from the book to read, for whom it acted as a useful way in. They argued over it. Was her focus on segregated lifestyles unnecessarily dismissive of other, younger, more integrated metropolitan strands of Britishness that they knew? Was she patronising to working-class lifestyles - or paying them much needed attention? They pointed out that these arguments might be used to talk about types of popular culture which do not feature in the book, and many related the experiences written about to their own. In short, it became a useful text to think with and from, in part because the text does not shy away from the complexity of the issues, and is not in search of easy answers.

The book raises many similar issues to *The Parekh Report on The Future of Multi-Ethnic Britain* (Profile Books 2000) upon which it might in some respects be thought to function as a more informal and discursive variant (Alibhai-Brown was part of the Commission on the Future of Multi-Ethnic Britain which preceded and fed into this document). Parekh's ideas are referred to early on, when Alibhai-Brown hopes that 'he will forgive me for taking his lofty thoughts and translating them into slightly more accessible form'. And the issue of accessibility is important, as her work is admirably and self-consciously populist, not by any means targeted solely at policy-making or academic institutions. If, on the one hand, her high public profile partly demonstrates the lack of imagination of journalists too lazy to expand their small pool of reliable non-white interviewees, on the other it shows the extent of her skill: at reaching a broad constituency, at being eloquently opinionated, at remaining knowledgeable about social, political and academic debates.

In terms of the theory it deploys, what is particularly impressive about *Who Do We Think We Are?* is how the strands of British cultural and political life are analysed through a committed anti-essentialism and an acute understanding of the complexities produced by a late capitalism which imagines itself to be postcolonial. Images of black and Asian people are slowly pulled into the mainstream of representation (what Stuart Hall has called 'multicultural drift'), not necessarily reflected in the establishment structures or life opportunities which are available. Its examples are sharp (for example, on the lack of status given to British black and Asian writers as opposed to their American peers), and when it promotes a parity of dialogue, rather than cultural tourism, it practises what it preaches ('this is not a book to explain us to you, nor you to them').

The only problematic section is that on 'the family'. Here the apparent lack of conceptual tools (particularly in terms of economic and political understanding) with which to discuss changes to the discourse of 'the family' breeds confusion:

why is there such turmoil over the family and about masculine and feminine roles in it? Is part of the problem that people talk too long and too hard about such issues? Could there be bliss in a little ignorance? [...] one major problem is that nothing [...] is left to individuals and their own instincts and inner life, strengths and beliefs. Too many experts seem to be cluttering up modern life.

This one chapter, then, falls back on a mode of individualist, liberal humanist analysis that the others become so impressive by both avoiding and critiquing. A better answer to this question of why there is such turmoil over family life could have integrated the previous chapter's analysis of changing gender roles alongside an understanding of how changes in global patterns of work and consumption have disrupted the relatively recent British conception of 'the family'. In addition, a fuller explanation of how she came to interview the people whose tales are scattered throughout the narrative as evidence would have provided a better understanding of her methodology.

But in the context of the rest of the book, these are relatively minor complaints. This is a work which combines investigative journalism with academic research, which combines social analysis with usefully targeted polemic. If the very act of asking the question 'who do we think we are?' implies a national identity or series of identities which are perhaps not so much 'in crisis' as 'in opportunity' - full of potential to be re-made - then this book is a significant gesture towards re-making them.

Soundings back issues

Issue 1 – Launch Issue – Stuart Hall on New Labour / Beatrix Campbell on communitarianism / Fred Halliday on the international order / Mae-Wan Ho on genetic engineering / Barbara Castle on Labour / Simon Edge on gay politics.

Issue 2 – Law & Justice, edited by Bill Bowring – contributors – Kate Markus, Keir Starmer, Ken Wiwa, Kader Asmal, Mike Mansfield, Jonathan Cooper, Ethan Raup, John Griffith, Keith Ewing, Ruth Lister and Anna Coote. Plus Steven Rose on neurogenetic determinism / Jeffrey Weeks on sexual communities / David Bell on Dennis Potter.

Issue 3 – Heroes & Heroines – contributors – Barbara Taylor, Jonathan Rutherford, Graham Dawson, Becky Hall, Anna Grimshaw, Simon Edge, Kirsten Notten, Susannah Radstone, Graham Martin and Cynthia Cockburn. Plus Anthony Barnett on Di's Divorce / David Donnison on New Labour / John Gill and Nick Hallam on Euro '96.

Issue 4 – The Public Good – edited by Maureen Mackintosh – contributors – Gail Lewis, Francie Lund, Pam Smith, Loretta Loach, John Clarke, Jane Falkingham, Paul Johnson, Will Hutton, Charlie King, Anne Simpson, Brigid Benson, Candy Stokes, Anne Showstack Sassoon, Sarabajaya Kumar, Ann Hudock, Carlo Borzaga and John Stewart. Plus Paul Hirst and Grahame Thompson on globalisation / Anne Phillips on socialism and equality / Richard Levins on critical science.

Issue 5 – Media Worlds – edited by Bill Schwarz and David Morley – contributors – James Curran, Sarah Benton, Esther Leslie, Angela McRobbie, David Hesmondhalgh, Jonathan Burston, Kevin Robins, Tony Dowmunt and Tim O'Sullivan. Plus Phil Cohen on community / Duncan Green on Latin America / Cynthia Cockburn on women in Israel.

Issue 6 – 'Young Britain' – edited by Jonathan Rutherford – contributors – Jonathan Keane, Bilkis Malek, Elaine Pennicott, Ian Brinkley, John Healey, Frances O'Grady, Rupa Huq, Michael Kenny and Peter Gartside. Plus Miriam Glucksmann on Berlin Memories / Costis Hadjimichalis on Europe / Joanna Moncrieff on psychiatric imperialism.

Issue 7 – States of Africa – edited by Victoria Brittain and Rakiya Omaar – contributors – Basil Davidson, Augustin Ndahimana Buranga, Kathurima M'Inoti, Lucy Hannan, Jenny Matthews, Ngugi Wa Mirii, Kevin Watkins, Joseph Hanlon, Laurence Cockcroft, Joseph Warioba, Vic Allen and James Motlasi. Plus Bill Schwarz on the Conservatives / Wendy Wheeler on 'uncanny families' / Dave Featherstone on 'Pure Genius'.

Issue 8 – Active Welfare – edited by Andrew Cooper – contributors – Rachel Hetherington and Helen Morgan John Pitts, Angela Leopold, Hassan Ezzedine, Alain Grevot, Margherita Gobbi, Angelo Cassin and Monica Savio. Plus Michael Rustin on higher education / Colette Harris on Tajikistan / Patrick Wright interview.

Issue 9 – European Left – edited by Martin Peterson – contributors – Branka Likic-Brboric, Mate Szabo, Leonadis Donskis, Peter Weinreich, Alain Caille, John Crowley, Ove Sernhede and Alexandra Alund. Plus Angela McRobbie on the music industry / Mario Petrucci on responsibility for future generations / Philip Arestis and Malcolm Sawyer on the new monetarism.

Issue 10 – Windrush Echoes – edited by Gail Lewis and Lola Young – contributors – Anne Phoenix, Jackie Kay, Julia Sudbury, Femi Franklin, David Sibley, Mike Phillips, Phil Cole, Bilkis Malek, Sonia Boyce, Roshi Naidoo, Val Wilmer and Stuart Hall. Plus Alan Finlayson on Labour and modernisation / Richard Moncrieff on the Ivory Coast / Mario Pianta on Italy.

Issue 11 – Emotional Labour – edited by Pam Smith – contributors – Stephen Lloyd Smith, Dympna Casey, Marjorie Mayo, Minoo Moallem, Prue Chamberlayne,

Rosy Martin, Sue Williams and Gillian Clarke. Plus Andreas Hess on individualism and identity/ T. V. Sathyamurthy on South Asia / Les Black, Tim Crabbe and John Solomos on 'Reggae Boyz'.

Issue 12 – Transversal Politics – edited by Cynthia Cockburn and Lynette Hunter – contributors - Nira Yuval-Davis, Pragna Patel, Marie Mulholland, Rebecca O'Rourke, Gerri Moriarty, Jane Plastow and Rosie. Plus Bruno Latour on the Left / Gerry Hassan on Scotland / Nick Jeffrey on racism in South East London.

Issue 13 – These Sporting Times – edited by Andrew Blake – contributors – Carol Smith, Simon Cook, Adam Brown, Steve Greenfield, Guy Osborne, Gemma Bryden, Steve Hawes, Alan Tomlinson and Adam Locks. Plus Geoff Andrews on New Labour / Fred Halliday on Turkey / Nick Henry and Adrian Passmore on Birmingham.

Issue 14 – One-Dimensional Politics – edited by Wendy Wheeler and Michael Rustin – contributors – Wendy Wheeler, Michael Rustin, Dave Byrne, Gavin Poynter, Barry Richards and Mario Petrucci. Plus Ann Briggs on Bullying / David Renton on South Africa / Isaac Balbus on the 1960s/ Laura Dubinsky on US trade unions.

Issue 15 – States of Mind – edited by Michael Rustin – contributors – Alan Shuttleworth, Andrew Cooper, Helen Lucey, Diane Reay, Richard Graham and Jennifer Wakelyn. Plus Nancy Fraser on the left/ Stephen Wilkinson on Cuba/ Mike Waite on social entrepreneurs/ Kate Young on violence against women in Bangladesh.

Issue 16 – Civil Society – edited by Andreas Hess – contributors – Jeffrey C. Alexander, Robert Fine, Maria Pia Lara, William Outhwaite, Claire Wallace, Grazyna Kubica-Heller, Jonathan Freedland. Plus Peter Howells on wealth and money/ G. C.Harcourt on compulsory voting/ Emma Satyamurti on living with difference/ Simon Lewis on South Africa/ Paulette Goudge on third world emergencies/ Tom Wengraf on Bourdieu.

Issue 17 – New Political Directions – edited by Michael Rustin and Doreen Massey – contributors – Sarah Benton on inclusive citizenship/ Giulio Marcon and Mario Pianta on Italian peace movements/ Massimo Cacciari interview/ Sue Tibballs on sex and the left/ Richard Minns on pensions and the capital market business/ Ian Taylor on the Canadian Right/ John Calmore on race in the US/ Judith Rugg and Michele Sedgwick on Budapest's statue park/ Ruby Millington on young offender institutions/ Merilyn Moos on her mother's life. Plus Jon Bloomfield, Nick Henry, Phil Hubbard, Kevin Ward and David Donnison on the future of cities.

Issue 18 – A Very British Affair – edited by Gerry Hassan – contributors – Gerry Hassan, Jim McCormick, Mark Perryman, Katie Grant, Cathal McCall, Charlotte Williams, Paul Chaney, John Coakley, Kevin Howard, Mary-Ann Stephenson, David T. Evans. Plus Hilary Wainwright, Angie Birtill, Beatrix Campbell, Jane Foot and Csaba Deak on cities and democracy/ Geoff Andrews on Berlusconi/ Glyn Ford on North Korea and Jane Desmarais on literature and anorexia.

SPECIAL ISSUE: THE NEXT TEN YEARS
Sarah Benton on people and government/ Anthony Barnett on constitutional reform/ Mary Hickman on Northern Ireland/ Ash Amin on regional inequality/ Jean Gardner on women / Tim Lang on food/ Kerry Hamilton and Susan Hoyle on transport/ Bill Bowring on law and order/ Gavi Poynter on unions/ Richard Wilkinson on health

All back issues cost £9.99, post-free. *The Next Ten Years* costs £7.99, post-free.

Send your orders to Soundings, Lawrence and Wishart, 99a Wallis Road, London E9 5LN. Or email to soundings@l-w-bks.demon.co.uk. Tel 020 8533 2506 Fax 020 8533 7369

Soundings

Described by the political theorist John Gray as a 'well written and welcome journal', Soundings is a unique venture that combines hard-edged political argument with a broad spectrum of cultural content. Recent highlights have included Stuart Hall, Jackie Kay, Gail Lewis, Mike Phillips and Lola Young on the significance of Windrush; Victoria Brittain and Basil Davidson on states of Africa; Chantal Mouffe on the third way; Angela McRobbie on the culture industries; and Bill Schwarz on the Tories; special themes have also included the European Left, Young Britain, One-Dimensional Politics and A Very British Affair.

SPECIAL OFFER TO NEW SUBSCRIBERS

First time individual subscribers are entitled to a
£25 subscription for the first year

Subscription rates 2002 (3 issues)

Individual subscriptions: UK £35.00   *Rest of the World* £45

Institutional subscriptions: UK £70.00   *Rest of the World* £80.00

To subscribe, send your name and address and payment (cheque or credit card), stating which issue you want the subscription to start with, to Soundings, Lawrence and Wishart, 99a Wallis Road, London E9 5LN.

OR you can e-mail us at
subscriptions@l-w-bks.demon.co.uk